Experiential Exercises in Organi... Theory & Design

Second Edition

H. Eugene Baker, III
Steven K. Paulson

THOMSON

SOUTH-WESTERN

Australia · Brazil · Canada · Mexico · Singapore · Spain · United Kingdom · United States

THOMSON

SOUTH-WESTERN

Experiential Exercises In Organization Theory & Design, Second Edition
H. Eugene Baker, III and Steven K. Paulson

VP/Editorial Director:
Jack W. Calhoun

Editor-in-Chief:
Dave Shaut

Senior Acquisitions Editor:
Joe Sabatino

Developmental Editor:
Michael Guendelsberger

Senior Marketing Manager:
Kimberly Kanakes

Content Project Manager:
Juli A. Cook

Technology Project Editor:
Kristen Meere

Manager of Technology, Editorial:
Vicky True

Manufacturing Coordinator:
Doug Wilke

Production:
Maggie Sears
Barbara Pavey

Printer:
Thomson-West
Eagan, MN

Art Director:
Tippy McIntosh

Cover Designer:
Craig Ramsdell
Ramsdell Design

Cover Images:
©PhotoAlto

Library of Congress Control Number:
2006922959

For more information about our products, contact us at:

Thomson Learning Academic
Resource Center

1-800-423-0563

Thomson Higher Education
5191 Natorp Boulevard
Mason, OH 45040
USA

Table of Contents

The exercises have all been tested in the authors' classes and are drawn from a variety of sources, including books created for other settings such as college classes on organizational behavior and organizational development and the management consulting profession. All of the exercises, which were created for related purposes, have been adapted specifically for the organization theory course.

In order to minimize the time necessary to become familiar with the exercises, they are presented in a uniform format. Once the instructor and students become familiar with the format, a minimal amount of time is necessary to assess the features of a given exercise. This format consists of three parts: (1) objectives of the exercise in terms of outcomes that can be expected to be attained by the class; (2) process in terms of the actual steps that the student should follow to successfully complete the exercise; and (3) feedback—a separate page that provides questions that allow for an individualized debriefing of the exercise for the student. In most cases, these items are presented with a range of requirements inasmuch as all of the exercises may be adjusted to conform to the specific objectives and teaching techniques used by the instructor.

The book is intended for junior, senior, and masters level courses in organization theory as traditionally taught in departments and colleges of business, education, and public administration. The exercises could also be adapted for use in courses in organizational behavior and organization development. In addition, the book is well suited for use in management training programs aimed at middle- and top-level managers.

Instructor's Resources

Instructor's Manual (ISBN: 0-324-36139-4). The Instructor's Manual to accompany this text contains practical information about each exercise to more effectively administer it in the classroom.

Web site (http://www.thomsonedu.com/management/baker). The Web site includes additional information and instructor resources to facilitate use of this text.

About the Authors

H. Eugene Baker III received his Ph.D. from the University of Florida. He is Professor of Management and Department Chair at the University of North Florida, Coggin College of Business, Jacksonville, Florida. His specialties in both teaching and research include the organizational entry process, organizational socialization, organizational control mechanisms, organizational behavior, and organization theory. He has a special interest in teaching pedagogy and the use of experiential teaching techniques. Professor Baker has published several articles in both academic and professional publications.

Steven K. Paulson is Blanche and Luther Coggin Professor of Management at the University of North Florida, Coggin College of Business, Jacksonville, Florida. His Ph.D. is from Iowa State University. His teaching interests include organizational theory, business ethics, and international business management. His research specialization is the area of interorganizational relationships with a focus on regional trade blocs. Dr. Paulson's publications appear in practitioner as well as academic journals.

Dedication

To our next generation:

Isabel Marie Baker
Alexi Paulson
Hannah Paulson
Kayla Paulson
Marina Paulson

Preface

The basic purpose of this second edition of *Experiential Exercises in Organizational Theory and Design* remains the same: to provide the student of business courses in organization theory with a set of classroom exercises which will help to illustrate and internalize the basic principles of the course. There is no other comparable book available, yet the experiential approach is widely used and considered to be very effective for this course material.

New and Updated Material

The book has been expanded from 30 to 39 exercises corresponding to an increase in the number of chapters from ten to thirteen. The new chapters cover recent developments in the field in three areas: (1) the international environment (trading blocs, comparative advantages, cultural metaphors); (2) interorganizational relationships (vendor selection, supply chain management) and (3) information technology (the balanced scorecard, electronic communication). In all, the book contains twelve new exercises along with twenty seven which were retained from the first edition. Several of the retained exercises were modified as a result of suggestions given by users of the book as well as our own classroom experiences. An example of this is the addition of a second exercise related to the Apple-Orange scenario where students are challenged to go beyond considering either a functional or a product structure to designing a matrix structure.

Organization of the Book

The chapters of the book continue to cover the most basic and widely covered topics of the field. Each chapter consists of a central focus, such as organizational structure, organizational power, or organizational culture, with all necessary materials to fully participate in three different exercises. The instructor's manual is a crucial document for the use of this book.

Taken together, the thirty nine exercises represent a wide variety in terms of time requirements: from less than five minutes to prepare to preparation requiring one hour or more; from very brief, ten-minute warm ups to exercises that could take an entire 50 to 75 minute class meeting period or longer. The settings range from the students' own college to fast food chains to large corporate entities; some exercises are intended to be completed at the level of the individual, others in groups, and still others can be used either way. The exercises range from instrumentation-based, using assessment questionnaires, to actual creative production activities. One new exercise (Exercise 12) enables students to make the connection between organizational structure and profit.

Chapter 1

Organizations and Organization Theory

Exercise 1—Connect the Numbers!

Exercise 2—Exchange Game

Exercise 3—You'll Play the Role So Why Not Pick the Part?

EXERCISE 1

Connect the Numbers!

I. Objectives:

This exercise is designed to (a) illustrate two commonly used approaches to solve management problems and (b) uncover the complementary relationship between using common sense to guide problem solving and using scientific theory and data to guide problem solving.

II. Process:

Step 1. Introduction

Problem solving and decision making pervade all areas of management. Regardless of whether the manager is making a decision about whom to promote, when to initiate a new product, or where to cut back the budget, the ultimate quality of the decision will depend on how the manager conducts the problem-solving process.

Step 2. Collection of numbers

Your instructor will provide you with a page containing a collection of numbers. The numbers range from the number one (1) to the number sixty (60). The number one (1) is in the upper left hand corner of the page.

Step 3. Connect the numbers

When told by your instructor to begin, connect the numbers in numerical order beginning with number one (1) and proceed until number sixty (60). You will be given a time for completing the task. Stop when instructed to do so.

Step 4. Discussion

Specific discussion topics will be provided by your instructor.

Exercise Feedback Form

Chapter 1—Exercise 1

Name: _____ **Student ID:** _____

1. The following facts about the data are

2. How can the numbers in the "problem" be represented?

3. How far did you get in "connecting the numbers" on the first try?

4. How far did you get on the second try? Why?

You may be asked to complete and turn in this form to your instructor.

EXERCISE 2

Exchange Game

I. Objective:

To develop an understanding of various processes involved in organizational management.

II. Process:

Step 1. Introduction

The instructions are self-explanatory and are provided on "Exchange Card Number 1." We will play three rounds. Detach the playing card for Round 1 (p. 9).

Step 2. Scoring Round 1

Calculate score for Round 1.

Step 3. Complete Round 2

Complete Round 2 according to instructions from your instructor.

Step 4. Score Round 2

Calculate score for Round 2

Step 5. Complete Round 3

Complete Round 3 according to instructions from your instructor.

Step 6. Score Round 3

Calculate score for Round 3

Step 7. Discussion

Discuss the various organizational techniques or practices that may have evolved as a result of the exercise.

Exchange Card Number 1

Object of the game: To accumulate as many points as possible within a fixed time limit.

Scoring: 1 point for every different signature on either side of the card you hold when time is called.

Rules: Your instructor will announce the beginning and ending of the playing time. You may only sign a card that you personally hold and control.

Exercise Feedback Form

Chapter 1—Exercise 2

Name: _____ **Student ID:** _____

1. Was the first round surprising? Why?

2. What ideas did you think of to increase your individual score?

3. How did the discussion of the exercise increase your awareness of the need to "organize"?

You may be asked to complete and turn in this form to your instructor.

EXERCISE 3

You'll Play the Role So Why Not Pick the Part?

I. Objectives:

To help reinforce an understanding of the practical distinctions among five organizational "parts" and to learn about the stereotypical perceptions which people hold about others who are involved in different functional areas of the company.

II. Process:

Step 1. Introduction

Thoroughly familiarize yourself with the five organizational parts.

Step 2. Your Preference

Rank the five organizational parts in decreasing order of your own personal preference for a major portion of your occupational career (i.e. #1 = highest preference, #5 = lowest preference) and, on the lines provided, provide a one-sentence explanation for the ranking.

1. _____

_____

_____

_____

_____

2. _____

_____

_____

_____

_____

3.

_____

_____

_____

4. _____

_____

_____

_____

5. _____

_____

_____

_____

Step 3. Group Formation

Based on your responses to the above questions, or another criterion, as directed by your instructor, you will be assigned to one of five groups. The groups may be equal in size, or they may be quite unequal in size. Regardless, however, each of the groups will correspond to one of the five organizational "parts." Your group will be located in an area of the classroom which is spatially separated from the others in a manner corresponding to the organizational chart. That is, the Top Management group should be located near the front of the classroom, the Technical Core in the back of the classroom and the Middle Management group centered between the two; the Technical Support group and Administrative Support Staff group should be located on the extreme right and left sides of the room respectively.

Step 4. Group Discussion

Although the exact assignment to the group will differ depending on the objectives of the course, the basic idea is to record (a) how you believe you would perceive your own organizational part and (b) as a member of this organizational part, how you believe you would perceive the other four organizational parts. Depending on your instructor's goals, these perceptions may focus on positive or negative attributes, cooperative or conflicting or calculative political or other focuses.

Step 5. Group Report

Select one of your group members to present the conclusions of your discussion. A very brief statement (1-5 words) should suffice for each one of the five perceptions. Note: past experience suggests that there may be derisive reactions to your statements (especially between staff and line units and between the Top Management group and all other units) but theory suggests that all functions are necessary so pay little attention to detractors!

Step 6. Class Discussion

Depending upon the objectives of the course, this exercise will point out different principles. Nevertheless, on the basis of your experience in this exercise, how easy do you believe it would be for people in different functional areas of a company to form inaccurate stereotypes of one another? How can these stereotypes be avoided? What other theories are relevant in this situation? Does TQM (Total Quality Management), for example, relate to these issues? Is organizational culture an important consideration?

Perceptions Scorecard

Your Part: _____

Perceptions held by your part about

Top Management: _____
_____
_____
_____

Middle Management: _____
_____
_____
_____

Technical Core: _____
_____
_____
_____

Technical
Support Staff: _____
_____
_____

Administrative
Support Staff: _____
_____
_____
_____

TOP MANAGEMENT

- Board of Directors
- President/CEO
- Executive Committee
- Chief Operating Officer

MIDDLE MANAGEMENT

- Vice President Operations
  - Manager Plant A
  - Manager Plant B
- Vice President Marketing
  - Manager Regional Sales
  - Manager Public Relations
- Vice President Physical Plant
  - Manager Human Resources
  - Manager Plant Operations

SUPPORT STAFF

- Supervisor Benefits
  - Benefits Clerk
  - Benefits Clerk
- Supervisor Facilities
  - Security Guard
  - Food Services

TECHNICAL CORE

- Supervisor District Sales
- Supervisor District Sales
  - Salesperson
  - Salesperson
- Supervisor Assembly
  - Fabricator
  - Assembler

TECHNICAL SUPPORT

- Supervisor Quality Control
  - Operations Research
  - Technician

Exercise Feedback Form

Chapter 1—Exercise 3

Name: _____ Student ID: _____

1. How accurate do you believe your perceptions of each "part" of the organization were? Why?

2. How accurate do you believe the perceptions of others of your part were? Why?

3. How might you reconcile the differences in perception?

You may be asked to complete and turn in this form to your instructor.

Chapter 2

Strategy, Organization Design, and Effectiveness

EXERCISE 4

When Is a Business Effective in the U.S. . . . .and Around the World?

I. Objectives:

To learn about an eight-level hierarchy of purposes which U.S. corporate executives hold for business enterprises and to compare such rankings with those of several different nations.

II. Process:

Step 1. Rank Order of Goals of Business Executives

In a series of cross-cultural studies, George W. England asked business executives to assess the relative importance of eight goals which are often mentioned as basic to business activity. Based on your general knowledge and intuition, place the numbers 1 through 8 in each column of "Form A" to indicate your opinion of the relative importance of the goals in the countries indicated; let 1 = most important and 8 = least important. Although some goals may seem similar, for the purpose of this exercise use only whole numbers and each number only once to indicate the rank order.

Step 2. Time Relevance and/or Group Consensus

Based on the objectives for the course, your instructor may ask you to fill in "Form B" with somewhat different instructions than those for Step 1.

Business Goals in Five Countries—Form A

Business Goals	Australia	India	Japan	Korea	U.S.A.
High Productivity					
Industry Leadership					
Employee Welfare					
Organizational Stability					
Profit Maximization					
Organizational Efficiency					
Social Welfare					
Organizational Growth					

Business Goals in Five Countries—Form B

Business Goals	Australia	India	Japan	Korea	U.S.A.
High Productivity					
Industry Leadership					
Employee Welfare					
Organizational Stability					
Profit Maximization					
Organizational Efficiency					
Social Welfare					
Organizational Growth					

Exercise Feedback Form

Chapter 2—Exercise 4

Name: _____ **Student ID:** _____

1. What surprised you most about the actual rankings of business executives? Why?

2. Why do you imagine that "Profit" was not consistently ranked number 1 in spite of the almost universal definition of business as a "profit seeking organization?"

3. What items do you believe should be added to the list of characteristics?

You may be asked to complete and turn in this form to your instructor.

EXERCISE 5

Fast Food and Effectiveness: An Organizational Diagnosis

I. Objectives:

To diagnose an organization in terms of goals, policies, procedures, structure, climate, technology, environment, job design, communication, and leadership, and to compare and contrast two organizations on these variables.

II. Process

Step 1. Introduction

A critical first step in improving or changing any organization is diagnosing or analyzing its present functioning. Many change and organizational development efforts fall short of their objectives because this important step was not taken, or was conducted superficially. To illustrate this, imagine how you would feel if you went to your doctor complaining of stomach pains, and the doctor recommended surgery without conducting any tests, without obtaining any further information, and without a careful physical examination. You would probably switch doctors! Yet managers often attempt major changes with correspondingly little diagnostic work in advance. In this exercise, you will be asked to conduct a group diagnosis of two different organizations in the fast food business. The exercise will provide an opportunity to integrate much of the knowledge you have gained in other exercises and in studying other topics. Your task will be to describe the organizations as carefully as you can in terms of several key organizational concepts. Although the organizations are probably very familiar to you, try to step back and look at them as though you were seeing them for the first time.

Step 2. Your Assignment

The group will be formed into subgroups. Your assignment is described as follows:

Your group, Fastalk Consultants, is known as the shrewdest but most insightful management consulting firm in the country. You have been hired by Mr. Bhik Maak, McDonald's President, to make recommendations for improving the motivation and performance of personnel in their franchise operations. Let us assume that key job activities in franchise operations are food preparation, order-taking and dealing with customers, and routine clean-up operations.

Recently Mr. Maak has come to suspect that his company's competitors such as Burger King, Wendy's, Jack in the Box, various pizza establishments, and others are making heavy inroads into McDonald's market. He has also hired a market research firm to investigate and compare the relative merits of the sandwiches, French fries, and drinks served in McDonald's and the competitor, and has asked the market research firm to assess the advertising campaigns of the two organizations. Hence, you will not need to be concerned with marketing issues, except as they may have an impact on employee behavior. The president wants you to look into the organization of the franchises to determine the strengths and weaknesses of each. Select a competitor who gives McDonald's a good "run for its money" in your area.

Mr. Maak has established an unusual contract with you. He wants you to make your recommendations based upon your observations as a customer. He does not want you to do a complete diagnosis with interviews, surveys, or behind-the-scenes observations. He wants your report in two parts.

A. Given his organization's goals of profitability, sales volume, fast and courteous service, and cleanliness, he wants an analysis that will compare and contrast McDonald's and the competitor in terms of the following concepts:

Organizational goals
Organizational structure
Technology
Environment
Employee motivation
Communication
Leadership style
Policies/procedures/rules/standards
Job design
Organizational climate

B. Given the corporate goals listed under point A above, what specific actions might McDonald's management and franchise owners take in the following areas listed below to achieve these goals (profitability, sales volume, fast and courteous service, and cleanliness)?

Job design and workflow
Organizational structure (at the individual restaurant level)
Employee incentives
Leadership
Employee selection

Step 3. Initial Assessment

How do McDonald's and the competitor differ in these aspects? Which company has the best approach?

Step 4. Some guidelines

A. Substantiate your recommendations by reference to one or more theories of motivation, leadership, small groups, or job design.

B. The president wants concrete, specific, and practical recommendations. Avoid vague generalizations such as "improve communications" or "increase trust." Say very clearly how management can improve organizational performance.

C. As you make your group presentation, the rest of the group will play the role of the top management executive committee. They may be a bit skeptical. They will ask tough questions. They will have to be sold on your ideas.

D. You will have 10 minutes in which to present your ideas to the executive committee and to respond to their questions.

Step 5. Outside of Class Preparation

Complete the assignment by going as a group to one McDonald's and one competitor's restaurant. If possible, have a meal in each place. To get a more valid comparison, visit a McDonald's and a competitor located in the same area. After observing each restaurant, meet with your group and prepare your 10-minute report to the executive committee.

Step 6. Class Report

In class, each subgroup will present its report to the rest of the group, who will act as the executive committee. The group leader will appoint a timekeeper to be sure that each subgroup sticks to its 10-minute time limit.

Exercise Feedback Form

Chapter 2—Exercise 5

Name: _____ **Student ID:**_____

1. Look again at the items of the "A" list in Step 2 of the process section of the exercise. Which one of these items was the most difficult to document? Why? Which one was the easiest to document? Why?

2. After participating in this exercise, have your perceptions of fast food restaurants become somewhat different? Why or why not?

3. How do you believe that other retail stores would compare to those in the fast food industry? Would there be very large differences? Why or why not?

You may be asked to complete and turn in this form to your instructor.

EXERCISE 6

Strategy, Stakeholders, and Social Responsibility

I. Objectives:

To become familiar with the four strategic positions described by Miles and Snow, to experience zero-sum decision making as individuals or as members of groups, to develop an awareness of various stakeholder groups which are relevant to financial decisions of manufacturing organizations in the community and to experience the complexity of making operational and financial decisions with an awareness of the social responsibility of the firm.

II. Process:

Step 1. Exercise Scenario

You are the plant manager (or a member of the Plant Management Group) for a small manufacturing plant which has developed (i.e. the instructor has assigned) one particular strategic approach (defender, prospector, reactor or analyzer). You have the authority to allocate funds, as you deem appropriate. However, you also must be able to justify your decisions to top management, your employees, the community, and other interested people from the perspective of the strategic approach which has been developed (assigned). Although the plant has been operating at an acceptable level, there is always the need to improve operations. You have argued that with extra funding, you could make significant improvements in the plant's operations. The company has given you the opportunity to prove the merit of your ideas by allocating an additional $1 million to your budget. There are some constraints, as follows:

1. You must spend the money for the projects listed below in Step 2.

2. You must spend, for each project, at least the amount listed under the first column (from the left) and you may spend only the amounts listed.

3. You may have to justify your allocation decisions to a committee of managers, employees, and other members of the business community. These decisions must be consistent with the strategic approach you have been assigned.

4. Any money you do not spend must be returned to the parent company and is lost to you.

Step 2. Complete worksheet

Consider the alternatives on the Allocation Categories figure.

Step 3. Make decisions concerning financial allocations.

Market Research: $ _____

Dividends: $ _____

Wage Increases: $ _____

Pollution Control: $ _____

Discrimination: $ _____

Research and Development: $ _____

Enhance Public Image: $ _____

Compensation: $ _____

       Total: $ _____

Exercise Feedback Form

Chapter 2—Exercise 6

Name: _____ **Student ID:** _____

1. Even though this exercise was fictitious, did certain decisions make you feel personally uncomfortable? Why or why not?

2. How much influence did financial allocation restrictions, such as the need to budget exactly $1,000,000, have on your decisions?

3. If you could select any one of the four strategic orientations to follow in your business career, which one would it be? Why?

You may be asked to complete and turn in this form to your instructor.

Allocation Categories

Projects	Alternative A	Alternative B	Alternative C
Market research market share	Maintain current national market Cost $50,000	Study penetration of international business Cost $200,000	Explore options Cost $300,000
Dividends	Pay none Cost $0	Pay $.50 per share Cost $150,000	Pay $1 per share and attract investors Cost $300,000
Wage increases	Maintain current levels Cost $0	5% cost of living increase Cost $150,000	Cost of living and 5% merit Cost $300,000
Pollution control	Kill everything within 1 mile Cost $0	Comply with new legislation Cost $150,000	Significantly reduce pollution Cost $250,000
Discrimination	Hire qualified white males and risk a discrimination suit Cost $140,000	Hire a few minorities and hope for the best Cost $250,000	Hire "hard core" unemployed and train and generate much goodwill Cost $350,000
Research and development	Leave well enough alone Cost $0	Research means of reducing manufacturing costs Cost $150,000	Seek ways to increase brand loyalty Cost $250,000
Enhance public image	Host wine and cheese party for local officials Cost $10,000	Hold weekend retreat for major stockholders Cost $150,000	Rent resort for a week to gain support of major financial institutions Cost $250,000
Compensation	Money is unimportant Pay self $0	Pay self $50,000 in salary and fringe benefits	Pay self $100,000

Chapter 3

Fundamentals of Organization Structure

EXERCISE 7

The Apple-Orange Company Structure—Part I

I. Objective:

To stimulate thinking about the fact that there are several different ways to organize work.

II. Process:

Step 1. Introduction

Read the description of the Apple-Orange Company. When you have finished, answer the questions that follow.

THE APPLE-ORANGE COMPANY

The Apple-Orange Company grows and markets apples and oranges in the southeastern United States. Apple-Orange has been in the produce business for the past 50 years and has some of the finest land for growing these fruits. They have also been quite successful in marketing their products. Up until now, Apple-Orange has been a family business run by old John Graves, whose father and uncle started the business. He has had his son Carl working as his assistant since Carl returned from Vietnam.

Basically three major sets of activities must be accomplished to grow and market Apple-Orange's products. One group of workers and managers work in the fields, handling the growing and harvesting of the apples and oranges.

Another group of workers and managers work in development research. This group is comprised largely of agricultural scientists who attempt to improve the varieties grown and to increase crop yield.

Marketing is handled by several sales personnel who call on wholesalers and fruit distributors in the region. The sales staff is very large and has been, like all other employees, very effective.

John and Carl have been managing Apple-Orange without many formal policies and procedures. The company has few set rules, procedures, and job descriptions. John believes that once people know their job, they should and would do it well.

However, Apple-Orange has grown fairly large and John and Carl both believe that it is now necessary to develop a more formal organization structure. They have invited D.J.

Blair, a noted management consultant, to help them. D.J. has told them that they have, basically, two choices. One is a functional organization structure and the second is a product-based organization structure. These two different forms are shown in the figure on the next page.

Step 2. Discussion Questions

Based on your own knowledge, guesses, and common sense, do you believe it is possible to "mix apples and oranges" in this case? That is, would your choice of structure be functional or product-based? Why do you prefer this structure for the case?

Is your choice Functional? Product-based? Why?

_____

_____

_____

_____

_____

_____

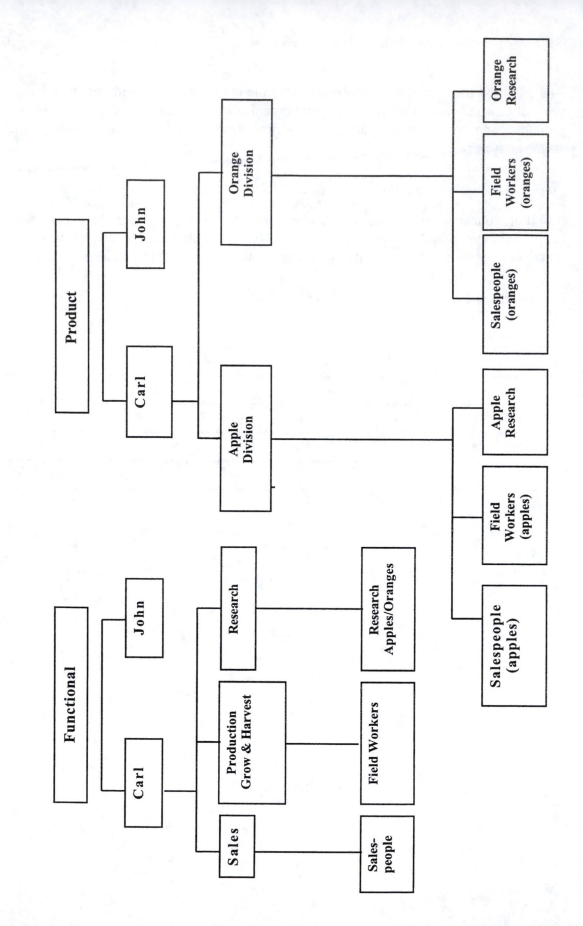

Exercise Feedback Form

Chapter 3—Exercise 7

Name: _____ **Student ID:** _____

1. What are some of the advantages of retaining the current structure of the company?

2. What are some of the advantages of implementing a functional structure? The disadvantages?

3. What are some of the advantages of implementing a product-based structure? The disadvantages?

You may be asked to complete and turn in this form to your instructor.

EXERCISE 8

The Apple-Orange Company Structure—Part II

I. Objective:

To encourage students to consider combining product-based and functional structures in the form of a matrix as an extension of the structural alternatives provided in Exercise 7.

II. Process:

Step 1. Introduction

Exercise 7 provided two alternative structural solutions to the dilemma faced by the Apple-Orange Company. This exercise provides an opportunity to design a third structure for the company as a combination of the function and product-based structures in the form of a matrix.

Step 2. The Apple-Orange Company

Reread the description of the Apple-Orange Company in Exercise 7.

Step 3. Draw the Chart

Draw an organization chart which includes elements of the functional structure and the product-based structure in the form of a matrix

Step 4. Discussion

Specific discussion instructions will be provided by your instructor.

Exercise Feedback Form

Chapter 3—Exercise 8

Name: _____ **Student ID:** _____

1. What seem to be the advantages of a matrix structure solution to the dilemma faced by the Apple Orange Company?

2. What are the disadvantages of a matrix solution?

3. How would it be possible to design a structure that includes some elements in a matrix and other elements in a functional system?

You may be asked to complete and turn in this form to your instructor.

EXERCISE 9

The Club Ed Exercise

I. Objective:

To explore structural alternatives and organizational systems options that are available to aid in the design and redesign of a changing organization.

II. Process:

Step 1. Introduction

Read the following scenario:

Determined never to shovel snow again, you are establishing a new resort business on a small Caribbean island. The building of the resort is under way and it is scheduled to open a year from now. You decide it is time to draw up an organizational chart for this new venture, Club Ed. What jobs do you need to have covered? What tasks need to be done? What services will you provide? Work in small groups to draw your organization chart and be prepared to present your design and to answer the following questions: What should it include? Why should it look like this?

Step 2.   Presentation of Design

Your instructor will select one or two groups to present their designs and lead the class discussion.

Step 3. Subsequent Designs

Your instructor will provide you with additional information that must be integrated into your decision and design process. You will be provided with time to develop a response.

Step 4. Class discussion

One or two groups will be selected to present their responses.

Exercise Feedback Form

Chapter 3—Exercise 9

Name: _____ **Student ID:** _____

1. How does the nature of an organization's technology influence organization design?

2. How can we measure the effectiveness of Club Ed? How does feedback about effectiveness influence organization design?

3. How can Club Ed structure itself as an adaptive organization? Does it always have to react to environmental changes or are there some ways it can be proactive?

You may be asked to complete and turn in this form to your instructor.

Chapter 4

The External Environment

EXERCISE 10

Diagnosis of Organizational Structure and Environmental Fit

I. Objective:

To use organizational theory as a basis for diagnosing and making recommendations concerning the fit between the environment of an organization and the internal structure of that organization.

II. Process

Step 1. Complete questionnaire

When assigned by the instructor, answer the questions in Parts I, II, and III.

Step 2. Compute Summary Score

PART I: Environmental Uncertainty (EU)

	To little or no extent	To a slight extent	To a moderate extent	To a considerable extent	To a very great extent
To what extent . . .					
. . .does the government frequently develop requirements, regulations, and policies that directly affect your organization?	☐	☐	☐	☐	☐
. . .do frequent technological changes or advances make current products or operations obsolete, requiring major changes?	☐	☐	☐	☐	☐
. . .is there intense competition among organizations in your field?	☐	☐	☐	☐	☐
. . .do different clients of your organization require individualized attention?	☐	☐	☐	☐	☐
. . .does the environment your organization operates in change unpredictably?	☐	☐	☐	☐	☐
Add up the checks in each column:					
Multiply as indicated:	x 1	x 2	x 3	x 4	x 5
Add: EU = _____ =	+	+	+	+	

PART II: Structural Complexity (SC)

	To little or no extent	To a slight extent	To a moderate extent	To a considerable extent	To a very great extent
To what extent . . .					
. . .do different groups or units operate on very different time lines (e.g., long-range versus short-term)?	☐	☐	☐	☐	☐
. . .do different groups or units in this organization have quite different task goals (as opposed to many groups doing the same or similar things)?	☐	☐	☐	☐	☐
. . .do groups or units in this organization differ in terms of their emphasis or concern for people versus concern for getting the job done?	☐	☐	☐	☐	☐
. . .do groups or units differ in how formal things are (e.g., emphasis on adherence to rules, regulations, and policies, following the chain of command, etc., vs. few formal rules, much informal contact, etc.)?	☐	☐	☐	☐	☐
. . .are there many different specialized units, groups, or departments in this organization?	☐	☐	☐	☐	☐
Add up the checks in each column:					
Multiply as indicated:	x 1	x 2	x 3	x 4	x 5
Add: SC = _____ =	+	+	+	+	

PART III: Structural Formalization (SF)

	To little or no extent	To a slight extent	To a moderate extent	To a considerable extent	To a very great extent
To what extent . . .					
. . .are rules and policies an important basis for inter-unit coordination?	☐	☐	☐	☐	☐
. . .are formal plans a major basis for inter-unit coordination?	☐	☐	☐	☐	☐
. . .are formal liaisons (individuals or teams) a significant basis for inter-unit coordination?	☐	☐	☐	☐	☐
. . .are regular meetings and problem-solving sessions for mutual adjustment an important basis for inter-unit coordination?	☐	☐	☐	☐	☐
. . .is a great deal of formal effort devoted to inter-unit coordination?	☐	☐	☐	☐	☐
Add up the checks in each column:					
Multiply as indicated:	x 1	x 2	x 3	x 4	x 5
Add: SF =_____ =	+	+	+	+	

PART I: ENVIRONMENTAL UNCERTAINTY (EU) = _____

PART II: STRUCTURAL COMPLEXITY (SC)= _____

PART III: STRUCTURAL FORMALIZATION (SF) = _____

Scores range from 5 to 25 on each scale:

HIGH = 20-25

MODERATE   = 11-19

LOW = 5-10

Step 3. Discussion

Instructor will provide discussion issues.

Exercise Feedback Form

Chapter 4—Exercise 10

Name: _____ **Student ID:** _____

1. How many class members have organizations with EU-SC-SF "fit"?

2. What were the most common types of "mis-fit"? Why?

3. How would you go about reducing the SC score? Is it easier to change the SC score than it is to change the SF score? Why? Why not?

You may be asked to complete and turn in this form to your instructor.

EXERCISE 11

Stakeholder Demands

I. Objectives:

To understand that many factors outside the organization that a great impact on decisions made inside the organization, to realize that most of these factors evolve as the result of interaction between groups with differing views, and to develop the ability to consider the views of several external factors or "stakeholders" while maintaining a primary focus on the organization itself.

II. Process:

Step 1. Exercise Familiarization

After your instructor has assigned a case issue and a position to take (A, B or sometimes C), read the provided issue case scenario carefully.

Step 2. General Strategy

Work in groups or individually, as the instructor assigns, and decide upon a general philosophical approach to presenting your position on the issue.

Step 3. Specific Arguments

Develop a series of specific arguments based on the general strategy developed in Step 2. and record these according to the instructions of the instructor.

ISSUE CASE SCENARIOS

Issue Case 1

Due to a number of recent injuries and deaths of children a number of consumer groups have demanded that toy companies recall a number of products and institute a new safety testing program for all of these products. The toy companies respond that they do have a large testing and safety program now. They further state that all of their products are clearly labeled with the age group that is appropriate for the toy, safety instructions, and a toll-free telephone number that consumers can call with problems and suggestions. They note that the majority of injuries have occurred when the instructions were not followed or the toys were given to children younger than the age noted on the package.

    A. Consumer Group View

    B. Toy Industry View

Issue Case 2

During contract negotiations the union insists that now that the company is in good financial condition the employees must have a large wage increase to close the gap created by previously limiting increases to allow the company to recover its financial health. The company states that, although its condition has improved, if this large wage increase is approved it will no longer be able to be competitive in its pricing and will again face financial hardship.

    A. Union View

    B. Company View

Issue Case 3

One governmental regulatory agency is supporting legislation that will require additional safety restraints in automobiles while another agency is demanding increased mileage and reduced air pollution. The automobile manufacturers argue that these additional regulations, in addition to those already in effect, will have a disastrous effect on the industry by increasing the initial

cost of automobiles and their maintenance costs. In addition to increasing unemployment resulting from reduced sales, such regulations will reduce the number of families who will be able to afford a car.

    A. Government View

    B. Automobile Industry View

Issue Case 4

A large insurance company is under fire by several groups who have noted that although the company's work force is 70% female, none of the senior management positions are held by women. The groups state that if some action is not taken to rectify this problem they will start a nationwide boycott of the company. In the past this type of boycott has worked very well for the groups. The company maintains that it has made every effort to find women for senior management positions but has not been able to. The vast majority of women employed by the firm are in clerical positions. Although they have several educational programs to encourage their employees to become prepared for management positions, these programs are only a few years old and it will be several years before those participating in the programs will be ready to move into senior management.

A. Women's Group View

B. Insurance Company View

Issue Case 5

Local environmental agencies have filed notice with the local steel mill that it can no longer dump its waste into the river which serves as the town's source of drinking water. Some of the pollutants have been linked with increased cancer in the area. The mill's managers argue that this requirement to find a new method of waste disposal would increase operating costs so much that, given the strong foreign competition, they would have to close the mill. The local people say that the mill is the major employer in town and if the mill is closed over half the population will be unemployed. They would rather have jobs and bad water than no jobs.

A. Environmental Agency view

B. Steel Mill View

C. Employee View

Issue Case 6

Several airlines serving the same regional area have suggested that they agree on fares for certain routes. If they continue the current fare war they will not be able to continue service to several areas since only certain routes are profitable enough to continue under such low fare levels. The people in the towns which may no longer have service strongly support this idea. The government agencies involved are clear that such an agreement on price is illegal. If any attempt to fix fares is made they will fine the airlines involved.

A. Airline View

B. Government View

C. Local Town View

Step 4. Position Summary

Issue Case #1.   **Circle one: Position A B**

Discuss the General Strategy and Specific Arguments you or your group developed.

Issue Case #2.   **Circle one: Position A B**

Discuss the General Strategy and Specific Arguments you or your group developed.

Issue Case #3.   **Circle one: Position A B**

Discuss the General Strategy and Specific Arguments you or your group developed.

Issue Case #4.   **Circle one: Position A B**

Discuss the General Strategy and Specific Arguments you or your group developed.

Issue Case #5.   **Circle one: Position A B C**

Discuss the General Strategy and Specific Arguments you or your group developed.

Issue Case #6.   **Circle one: Position A B C**

Discuss the General Strategy and Specific Arguments you or your group developed.

Exercise Feedback Form

Chapter 4—Exercise 11

Name: _____ **Student ID:** _____

1. What difficulties did you experience when you were developing views for stakeholder groups?

2. Many types of stakeholders are illustrated in this exercise. Describe two additional types of stakeholders that business managers might have to take into account that are not illustrated by the exercise.

3. Identify any one of the issue cases which you were assigned in the exercise and the stakeholder view that you personally would feel most comfortable with. Why would you feel most comfortable with this view?

You may be asked to complete and turn in this form to your instructor.

EXERCISE 12

Environmental Domain and Profit

I. Objectives:

To challenge students to consider profit as a basic, universal element in the domain of all business organizations and the relative importance of organic and mechanistic structures for enhancing profitability of the firm.

II. Process:

Step 1. Introduction

An organization's domain consists of those claims which the organization deliberately stakes out for itself. For business organizations there is one domain element that may be considered universal and that is the striving to achieve a profit.

Step 2. The definition of business profit

Consider a manufacturing firm and describe how an accountant would calculate operating profit.

Step 3. Compare organic and mechanistic structures

List four essential characteristics of an organic structure and four essential characteristics of a mechanistic structure.

Step 4.   Profit and structure.

Consider the characteristics of organic and mechanistic firms which you listed in Step 3 and decide which type of structure would be more likely to enhance the profitability of the firm as you defined profit in Step 1.

Step 5. Discussion

Specific discussion instructions will be provided by your instructor.

Exercise Feedback Form

Chapter 4—Exercise 12

Name: _____ Student ID: _____

1. How would an accountant calculate operating profit? What are four essential characteristics of an organic structure and what are four essential characteristics of a mechanistic structure?

2. Based upon your answers to question 1, which one of the two structures, organic or mechanistic, do you believe would be the more likely to enhance profitability? Why?

3. How might organic and mechanistic structural characteristics be combined to achieve greater profitability than would be possible with exclusive use of either organic or mechanistic?

You may be asked to complete and turn in this form to your instructor.

Chapter 5

Interorganizational Relationships

EXERCISE 13

Grocery Store Dilemma

I. Objective:

To explore the relative merits of three different approaches to developing cooperative relationships among competing businesses in order to successfully compete against a common external threat to their individual markets.

II. Process:

Step 1. The Scenario

The instructor will assign you to one of the three grocery stores which are described in the following "Small Town Scenario." Read the entire "Small Town Scenario" concerning the situation facing your grocery store and the two other grocery stores in a small town.

Small Town Scenario

You live and work in a small town with three very competitive, small, locally owned grocery stores facing survival-threatening competition from a large supermarket chain which plans to build a super-supermarket in the center of town. You are part of the ownership group of one of these grocery stores; your group has decided to establish an interorganizational relationship with one or both of the other stores as a means of reducing uncertainty yet your organization wants to retain as much of the decision-making autonomy as possible. You hire a consultant who has reduced the relative "payoffs" of alternative courses of Interorganizational Relations (IOR) actions. Soon, a member of your group will meet with representatives of both of the other stores and then privately with the representative of each of the stores; thus three negotiations in which you will agree to some form of IOR. The three stores are as follows: Americana Grocery Store specializes in fresh produce but also sells meat and grocery items; Buddy's Grocery Store specializes in locally butchered meat but also sells produce and grocery items; Corner Grocery Store specializes in gourmet and ethnic specialty grocery items but also sells produce and meat. Note that "specializes" means a long tradition of low prices, high quality and much variety because of personal relationships outside of the organization and technical knowledge of the owners.

Step 2. The Payoff

Familiarize yourself with the following IOR Payoff Schedule.

    A.   If your store is not included in any mutual IOR ==> 0 points

B. If your store is included in a mutual dyadic IOR:

    contract   ==>   15 points
    cooptation   ==>   12 points
    coalition   ==>   9 points

C. If your store is included in a mutual triad IOR:

    contract   ==>   10 points
    cooptation   ==>   8 points
    coalition   ==>   6 points

Step 3. The Decision

When the instructor asks you for your grocery store's decision, write the following sentence on a piece of paper and fill in the blanks without consulting any other store. "Our store, the _____, hereby agrees to enter into a _____ type of interorganizational relationship with _____ for the purpose of decreasing competitive uncertainty while maintaining a degree of autonomy."

Exercise Feedback Form

Chapter 5—Exercise 13

Name: _____   **Student ID:** _____

1. How could the rules of the exercise be modified to allow for more trust among the three stores? Would this have made the IOR negotiation easier?

2. If the rules of the exercise had allowed for more complex forms of IOR to be designed, what might one of those have been?

3. Are you aware of a real situation that is similar to the small town scenario of this exercise? How did that situation work out? What form(s) of IOR were involved?

You may be asked to complete and turn in this form to your instructor.

EXERCISE 14

Survival of the Fittest

I. Objectives:

To enable students to think critically about the selection of interorganizational partners and to be able to identify common elements in this determination such that the firm that has the best "fit" is the one which will "survive" the selection process.

II. Process:

Step 1. Introduction.

Assume that you are a manager who is responsible for providing input on potential strategic alliance partners. The following paragraphs describe three potential partners with whom you might form a strategic alliance. Read each scenario and then answer the questions in Step 2.

The Alpha, Beta and Omega Companies

Alpha has had a long history of prior dealings with your firm. Alpha has been quick to respond to your inquiries and is willing to accommodate your needs (e.g., schedule changes). Many times over the years, Alpha's people have gone well above and beyond the call of duty to look out for your firm's interests. With your firm in particular, Alpha has really shown they value their relationship. Alpha has a reputation for being fair with partners and customers. For various reasons, you sometimes wonder if Alpha's employees are really as skilled as the industry seems to assume. You recently spoke with several of Alpha's customers. Two of their customers complained that Alpha's newly released product, although it worked, included some features that were poorly designed. A manager from another company said that they were having some problems with Alpha's products. In trying to resolve these problems, engineers from the manager's company felt that the Alpha employees did not have the necessary technical background to resolve the problems.

Beta has partnered with your firm for several years. You have been involved in managing this relationship for the past year. It is well known in your firm that Beta takes good care of your firm, going well beyond any contractual obligations to protect your firm's interests. Beta performs technical services that require that they be up-to-date. Beta keeps its knowledge current by sending employees to technical conferences and ensuring that they have access to technical journals. Beta's work has always been careful and complete.

Beta has shown great loyalty to you, a valued partner. For example, just last month a Beta manager blocked information from getting to your board of directors that would have made managers in your company look bad. Furthermore, Beta has shared competitive and technical information with you about your competitors and their products that Beta gained while partnering with them.

Omega is a firm with technical know-how that is widely regarded as state-of-the-art. The firm has a reputation for being fair and honest. Your firm has partnered with Omega for a number of years. The quality of their work has always been good. Omega has always fulfilled its contractual obligations and lived up to its agreements. However, Omega will not go beyond the strictly defined scope of the contract for your firm. You have a friend who is a manager at another firm that partners with Omega. Your friend tells you that Omega willingly and regularly performs extra tasks that are beyond the specifications in their contracts. You are aware that Omega has this type of close relationship with at least a few firms, but despite your firm's best efforts, you have been unable to develop a closer relationship with Omega.

Step 2. Fill out the questionnaire

Assess each potential partner on each of the eight statements by placing the values 1 through 4 in the boxes provided, where 1 = strongly disagree, 2 = disagree, 3 = agree, 4 = strongly agree.

	Alpha	**Beta**	**Omega**
1. Our company should partner with this firm.	☐	☐	☐
2. We would not have to keep an eye on this firm.	☐	☐	☐
3. This firm is very capable of performing its job.	☐	☐	☐
4. This firm is well qualified.	☐	☐	☐
5. Sound principles seem to guide this firm's actions.	☐	☐	☐
6. This firm will stick to its word.	☐	☐	☐
7. This firm will go out of its way to help our firm.	☐	☐	☐
8. This firm would not try to hurt our company.	☐	☐	☐
Totals	____	____	____

Step 3. Analyze the results

Add the numbers in each column (Alpha, Beta, Omega).

Step 4. Discussion

Specific discussion instructions will be provided by your instructor

Exercise Feedback Form

Chapter 5—Exercise 14

Name: _____   **Student ID:** _____

1. Which firm received your highest (most favorable) score? Which firm received your lowest (least favorable) score? Which questions made the biggest difference in the total scores?

2. What underlying criteria did you seem to use to assign values to the potential interorganizational partners?

3. What other questions could you ask to differentiate among the firms in terms of their fit for interorganizational partnership?

You may be asked to complete and turn in this form to your instructor.

EXERCISE 15

Friends and Foes in the Supply Chain

I. Objective:

To encourage students to conceptualize relations between purchasers and suppliers as potential networks of collaborators rather than battlefields of adversaries and to become familiar with the "4C" Sourcing Strategy as developed by Peter Grittner ("Four Elements of Successful Sourcing Strategies," *Management Review*, October 1996, 41-45).

II. Process:

Step 1. Introduction.

The traditional model for the interorganizational relationship between purchasers and suppliers in the supply chain is adversarial involving closed doors and treachery. Recent research indicates, however, that a more successful model is collaborative. In this exercise you are asked to become familiar with the "4C" model and then to identify elements of the model in five scenarios.

Step 2. The "4C" Sourcing Strategy

The "4C" sourcing strategy: Select a competitive supplier, establish a commitment to that supplier, analyze the complete manufacturing process with a cost-analysis mind-set and coordinate with the supplier early and often to maximize cost-efficiency.

- Competitive Suppliers: Working with a small number of select suppliers is not only possible, but smart. But relying on one or two suppliers for what used to be purchased from five or six also increases a company's risk, if it does not choose well. To evaluate suppliers, ask: Is the company competitive? Where does it rank in its industry?

- Commitment: Commitment can involve trusting the supplier with proprietary technology and other sensitive information and it is a choice that can offer high return. When a manufacturer makes a real commitment to its supplier, the supplier then can be encouraged to make a commitment in return by investing in the manufacturer's business and product.

- Cost-Analysis Mind-Set: A way of thinking about supplier economics: What drives their material costs, production cycles and staffing patterns? What affects their inventory and other carrying costs? How do manufacturers' product specifications and sourcing practices influence those costs?

- Coordination: Coordination involves developing cross-functional teams comprised of staff from both the supplier and the manufacturer and focusing on volume consolidation, dependable forecasting, product design, parts standardization and other overall cost-savings strategies that arise when a supplier and manufacturer sit around the same table as partners.

Step 3. Evaluate the Scenarios

For each of the following scenarios, select the sourcing strategy which you believe is most evident. Be prepared to defend your choice.

- **Story 1:** A New York equipment manufacturer decided to introduce a more analytical approach to its supply-chain management, with the goal of reducing procurement costs of filters, an important but expensive component. The New York firm was happy with the quality of its supplier's product, but felt it was paying too much for the part. A team of experts and managers was put together, visited the supplier and explained the study goal: to better understand the functions, activities and demands that added cost to the filter they built, and to explore potential avenues for reducing those costs. Based on a commitment from the manufacturer that the supplier would be a partner in the strategy and would share in any cost-savings measures that emerged, the supplier agreed to cooperate. The team toured the supplier's operation, tracking each step of the production process: raw materials cost, direct labor, equipment usage, set-up time, order processing, production planning and overhead costs. It became obvious that the direct-manufacturing costs were a fraction of the total product costs—about 30 percent. The other 70 percent was buried in the contribution margin supporting the indirect functions of marketing, developing, engineering, testing, packaging and shipping the New York firm's filter. But which indirect functions added the most cost, and why? To answer that question, the team met with engineering staff, production managers, quality inspectors and other personnel—including top management—involved in servicing the New York company. They learned that many of the indirect costs were attributable to two factors: erratic and inefficient ordering patterns and excessive and redundant post-production specifications for quality measurement and testing. By making long-term volume commitments, improving forecasting, coordinating order size and altering quality specifications that were inefficient or overlapping, the team was able to reduce total product costs from $7,300 to $4,000, a 46 percent savings.

- **Story 2:** A Wisconsin manufacturer makes scientific instruments with internal electronics. The firm outsourced the stuffing of its electronic boards to a built-to-print house with efficient, low-cost manufacturing and assembly capabilities. The supplier had no design or engineering resources, but the Wisconsin company was not looking for engineering help; it was hoping to get electronic boards outfitted cheaply. The design specs included an industry-standard capacitor, which the supplier was able to buy from one of three subsuppliers at 50 cents each. As industry standards changed, two of the capacitor makers moved on to different products, leaving only one subsupplier. In one year, the cost of the capacitor shot to $2 each, which the supplier had no choice but to pay in order to build the Wisconsin firm's product to spec. By the time the Wisconsin company took notice, the price of the obsolete capacitor had increased to $10 each and then production was discontinued altogether. Without electronic boards, the manufacturer's production came to a halt. It was unable to ship product for six months. A California-based competitor in the scientific instrumentation business also outsourced the stuffing of its electronics boards, but it selected a value-added supplier. Though the supplier quoted a higher initial price, it had a design and engineering team of more than a dozen people. The California company felt it was worth a small premium to do business with a supplier that had people trained and experienced to think about design and obsolescence issues in electronic components. It was right. When the number of capacitor suppliers fell from three to one, the value-added supplier predicted that the part would soon be obsolete and redesigned the board to accommodate a newer capacitor, priced at 50 cents. The design modifications were minor and inexpensive, and the California company's boards remained in continuous production at a competitive price, even when the original capacitor was discontinued.

- **Story 3:** An Ohio manufacturer purchased processed nickel for use in its lighting products and changed suppliers year to year based on the lowest bid for its product. During one stretch, it changed suppliers once a year for four years straight, confident that with each switch it was paying the lowest price for the product. A Massachusetts competitor took a different approach. After selecting a competitive supplier it felt comfortable with, it worked with the supplier to build an exclusive, long-term relationship. The Massachusetts firm promised the supplier 100 percent of its volume and a contract with no time limit, provided cost, quality and service didn't slip. The supplier, for its part, invested $19 million in a modernized furnace to provide its Massachusetts customer with state-of-the-art nickel processing. The new furnace allowed for faster annealing and wider nickel strips, and production costs fell dramatically. The manufacturer and its supplier shared in the savings. The Massachusetts competitor sustained a 16 percent cost advantage over the Ohio manufacturer over a period of six years, even though the supplier did not have the new plant operational until the fourth year.

- **Story 4:** A Kentucky engine manufacturer orders pumps from its supplier on an almost hourly basis, constantly changing scheduled orders and requiring fast expedition of the new order. As a result of the firm's erratic and piecemeal ordering practices, the supplier has to produce pumps in smaller, inefficient runs. A Connecticut competitor that buys from the same supplier better understands the supplier's manufacturing system—it produces pumps in economic lot sizes of 100 units, holding inventory at the component level before final assembly—and dependably forecasts larger orders based on optimal run lengths. The Connecticut firm also makes fewer adjustments to its orders once placed. The result? The Connecticut competitor pays $9,500 per unit versus the Kentucky firm's $10,700, enjoying a 13 percent savings per unit. By simply coordinating pump orders in larger quantities with a 90-day lead time, the Kentucky manufacturer could save $2.6 million per year.

- **Story 5:** A Midwestern manufacturer of medical systems buys $12.2 million worth of fabricated sheet metal from 35 vendors, purchasing metal pieces separately from lowest-priced vendors. This methodology is actually penny-wise but pound foolish: Its competitor coordinated with one supplier on design, resulting in fewer metal parts bundled in a 16-part kit. The competitor's better-engineered product used less metal due to fewer parts and reduced scrap based on the better fit of the designed kit. The simpler design also cut the vendor's labor costs: It required less time for assembly and eliminated welding steps. The result? While the Midwest manufacturer paid $550 per cabinet, the competitor paid $430, a 28 percent cost difference. By coordinating with a single-source supplier on cabinet design, the manufacturer would be able to realize annual savings of $2.4 million.

Step 4. Discussion

Specific discussion instructions will be provided by your instructor.

Exercise Feedback Form

Chapter 5—Exercise 15

Name: _____ **Student ID:** _____

1. Which one of the four sourcing strategies do you believe is most evident in story 1? Why?

2. Which one of the four sourcing strategies do you believe is most evident in story 2? Why?

3. Which one of the four sourcing strategies do you believe is most evident in story 3? Why?

4. Which one of the four sourcing strategies do you believe is most evident in story 4? Why?

5. Which one of the four sourcing strategies do you believe is most evident in story 5? Why?

You may be asked to complete and turn in this form to your instructor.

Chapter 6

The International Environment and Organization Design

EXERCISE 16

Poverty, Wealth, and Interfirm Trade

I. Objective:

To develop a greater awareness of the global environment that business organizations face today and that a major motivation for engaging in international business to business ("B2B") relationships is to obtain financial benefits of the comparative advantages which the firm has by virtue of the nation in which it resides. A secondary purpose of the exercise is to increase awareness of the comparative advantages of five trading blocs: the European Union, ASEAN, NAFTA, MERCOSUR and CARICOM.

II. Process:

Step 1. Introduction

A central principle of international trade theory is that two blocs of nations can increase their own levels of wealth by trading goods and services even though one of the blocs is not as efficient at producing any of the goods or services which are traded as the other country and the inefficient country has a lower GDP per capita. This exercise will illustrate this point if trading strategies are well thought out and negotiation skills are approximately the same.

Step 2. Group Formation

Your instructor will assign you to work with other members of the class as a group of decision makers in a firm located in a nation which belongs to one of these five trading blocs: The European Union, ASEAN, NAFTA, MERCOSUR and CARICOM.

Step 3. The International Scenario

You are a member of a business located in one of the following international trade groups which has a comparative advantage in the product noted in parentheses. The $US per capita GDP is also given in parentheses.

- The European Union (Autos—$20,889)

- ASEAN (Boats—$1,164)

- NAFTA (Corn—$27,670)

- MERCOSUR (Drums—$3,637)

- CARICOM (Ecotours—$2,462)

Your group starts with ten units of a good (conveniently labeled A,B,C,D,E). Each group should try to increase its wealth by trading goods with groups in other countries on a one-for-one basis; that is, if your group gives up one unit of A, your group gets one unit of B, or for two units of A you get two units of B, and so on. Your aim is to maximize your group's wealth.

Step 4. Trading Rules and Procedure

- Calculate the value of goods as follows:

#Units	Autos	Boats	Corn	Drums	Ecotours
1	$ 5,000	2,000	6,000	4,000	3,000
2	9,000	3,900	11,000	7,500	5,500
3	12,000	5,400	15,000	10,000	7,500
4	14,000	6,600	18,000	11,500	9,000
5	15,000	7,600	19,000	12,500	10,000
6	15,800	8,400	19,900	13,200	10,000
7	16,400	9,000	20,700	13,700	11,500
8	16,800	9,400	21,400	14,000	12,100
9	17,000	9,600	22,000	14,200	12,600
10	17,100	9,700	22,500	14,300	13,000

- The value of each unit of a good is a function of how much of that good you already own; that is, the more of any good that you have, the less each additional unit is worth. For example, one unit of A is worth $5,000; two units of A are worth $9,000, or $4,500 each.

- If your group gives up one unit you lose some value; this should be balanced against what you gain by trading. For example, if you have ten units of A and give one up you lose $100 (you go from ten units to nine, $17,100 to $17,000); if you trade for B and if you have no units of B you gain $2,000 (you go from zero units to one, $0 to $2,000). Your group gains $1,900. Alternatively, if you have six units of A and give one up, you lose $800 (you go from six units to five, $8,400 to $7,600); if you trade for B and if you have six units of B you gain $600 (you go from six units to seven, $8,400 to $9,000). Your country loses $200.

- You will have five minutes to discuss your strategy as an international trading bloc; you may decide to trade as individuals or as a group, but your gains or losses will accrue to the group. You will then trade, following your chosen strategy, with the other groups BUT ONLY in the room/area where one of the trading countries is located. Goods must be traded on a one-for-one basis only—if you give up one unit of a good you get one unit of another in return. Your objective is to maximize your group's wealth. Your instructor will tell you when to start trading and when to stop.

- You will recalculate your wealth at the end of the trading period and determine your gains or losses.

Step 5. Discussion

Specific discussion instructions will be provided by your instructor.

Exercise Feedback Form

Chapter 6—Exercise 16

Name: _____   **Student ID:** _____

1. Did your company increase its wealth by trading? Why or why not?

2. What was the strategy that your firm used to conduct trades with other firms? How would you change this strategy to increase your firm's success in a future round of trades? Why?

3. Even though firms in NAFTA and the European Union have an absolute advantage because of their greater initial wealth and access to financial resources, what enables firms in the other blocs also to increase their wealth?

You may be asked to complete and turn in this form to your instructor.

EXERCISE 17

International Metaphors

I. Objective:

To become familiar with the concept of cultural metaphor and its applications to organization design and to develop an understanding of one's own and others' organizational and national cultures through the development of cultural metaphors.

II. Process:

Step 1. Introduction.

This exercise involves the development of an understanding of the concept of cultural metaphor and an opportunity to develop a metaphor for the national culture of the United States and, depending upon the variation selected by the instructor, the culture of other nations as well as the cultures of specific business organizations.

Step 2. Review the Cultural Metaphor Concept

The cultural metaphor as developed by Martin Gannon (*Understanding Global Cultures: Metaphorical Journeys Through 28 Nations, Clusters of Nations and Continents.* Thousand Oaks, CA: Sage, 2004) is defined as a method for understanding easily and quickly the cultural mindset of a nation and comparing it to those of other nations. In essence, the method involves identifying some phenomenon, activity or institution of a nation's culture that all or most of its members consider to be very important and with which they identify cognitively and/or emotionally. The characteristics of the metaphor then become the basis for describing and understanding the essential features of the society.

As an example, Gannon presents the opera as a cultural metaphor for the nation of Italy. As he indicates, the Italians invented the opera and love it passionately. Five key characteristics of the opera are the overture, spectacle and pageantry, voice, externalization, and the interaction between the lead singers and the chorus. In addition to the Italian opera, Gannon identifies, among others, the German symphony, Belgian lace, the Spanish bullfight (which he distinguishes from the Portuguese bullfight) and the Irish conversation as cultural metaphors.

Step 3. Individual assignment: Create a cultural metaphor for the United States.

Select some aspect of the culture of the U.S. which you personally believe most of the members of the culture believe to be important and with which they identify.

Step 4. Group Formation

The instructor will assign students to groups of 3 to 6 people.

Step 5. Group Assignment: Create a cultural metaphor for the United States.

Based upon the discussion of the cultural metaphors developed by the members of the group, determine a single metaphor by consensus. Develop a report about your metaphor including (a) the name of the metaphor, (b) three important characteristics of this metaphor and, based upon these ideas, (c) three recommended guidelines for nonmembers of the U.S. culture to follow in their interactions with U.S. businesspeople.

Step 6. Presentation and Discussion

Specific group presentation and discussion instructions will be provided by your instructor.

Exercise Feedback Form

Chapter 6—Exercise 17

Name: _____ **Student ID:** _____

1. What is the cultural metaphor which you personally developed for the United States?

2. What is the cultural metaphor which your group developed for the United States?

3. Overall, how accurate do you personally believe that the group consensus metaphor is as a representation of the culture of the United States? Why?

EXERCISE 18

Global and Local: How to Have it All

I. Objective:

The primary objective of this exercise is to provide students with an opportunity to design a structure for a newly expanded international business organization. A secondary objective is to familiarize students with the concept of Foreign Trade Zone (FTZ) as a unique opportunity for an international firm to locate "outside" of the country ("global") while remaining completely domestic ("local").

II. Process:

Step 1. Introduction

For this exercise you will read a brief case description of an international manufacturing firm and then design a structure that will allow the firm to take advantage of a foreign trade zone so as to have advantages of both local and global operations or, in a sense, to "have it all."

Step 2. Moonbeam Electronics

Read the following case description of the Moonbeam Electronics company.

Moonbeam Electronics of Springfield, Missouri

Located in southwest Missouri, Moonbeam Electronics is a manufacturer of small electrical appliances, such as toasters, toaster ovens, can openers, mixers and blenders. Moonbeam assembles these products in its Springfield, Missouri, facility using a number of foreign suppliers for component parts. Virtually all products are assembled from parts from Japan, Taiwan, Korea and China. All of Moonbeam's production occurs in the Springfield facility and the company employs over 400 people. Although labor costs might be lower in Mexico or Asia, Moonbeam has never considered moving its production operations out of the country. Wages and benefit costs are moderate and the work force is productive. Moonbeam exports approximately 25% of its production to Latin America, Europe and Asia. The company hopes to increase its export potential with some product design changes and increased marketing efforts. Jim Harrison, vice president for logistics for Moonbeam, has been communicating with an old college friend who recently took a job at the Toyota production facility in Kentucky. Jim's friend told him that Toyota utilizes a foreign trade zone (FTZ) and that Moonbeam could benefit from one as well. After further discussions on the telephone, Jim decided to fly to

Kentucky to see the Toyota facility and learn more about the FTZ concept. Jim learned that Toyota imports from Japan component parts for its automobile manufacturing and that by utilizing an FTZ, the company avoids paying any customs duties on the component parts until the cars leave the FTZ. If the autos are exported out of the United States, then Toyota pays no tax on the component parts at all. It was explained to Jim that an FTZ is an area in the United States that is considered to be international territory and therefore U.S. customs duties do not apply. Jim has further learned that there are two types of foreign trade zones, a general-purpose trade zone and a subzone. The general-purpose trade zone operates for the benefit of several different companies and the subzone is established for one company's use exclusively. Toyota has a subzone for its production operations in Kentucky. From his visit, Jim has decided that there are three benefits to operating in an FTZ: (1) delay of payment of customs duties; (2) possible elimination of customs duties; (3) the bypassing of U.S. Customs regulations. He is confident that Moonbeam can realize all three benefits and would like to present a formal proposal to senior management to move operations from Springfield to a subzone of the FTZ in Kentucky. One of the key elements of his proposal will be a new organizational design. Jim has decided to recommend abandoning the current product structure in favor of a divisional structure which will have two divisions: "Domestic Division" and "International Export Division." Jim has learned that this type of structure is often referred to as a "domestic-international hybrid" design.

Step 3. Domestic-International Hybrid Design

Design a domestic-international hybrid organization structure which Moonbeam Electronics can use in the firm's new foreign trade zone location in Kentucky. Draw a chart which represents your design. Notice that because you have not been provided with details of the products and manufacturing processes, your design will be an overall plan rather than a specific operating guide.

Step 4. Discussion

Specific discussion instructions will be provided by your instructor.

Exercise Feedback Form

Chapter 6—Exercise 18

Name: _____ **Student ID:** _____

1. What are the advantages to Moonbeam Electronics of moving from a domestic product structure to a domestic-international hybrid structure?

2. What are the possible pitfalls of implementing the new organizational structure?

3. If the new structure is successful for the firm in terms of increased sales and decreased costs, what would you recommend as a next step in the expansion of the firm's operations? Why?

You may be asked to complete and turn in this form to your instructor.

Chapter 7

Manufacturing and Service Technologies

EXERCISE 19

Measuring Technology

I. Objective:

To assess the extent of task variability and problem analyzability present in various organizational units.

II. Process:

Task variability and problem analyzability can be measured in an organizational unit by answering the following ten questions. Scores are derived from responses scored on a one-to-seven scale for each question.

Step 1. Complete questionnaire

Complete the questionnaire for each of the following departments. Use the symbol for each department, i.e., Computer Operations—A, Methodology Department—B, etc.

(A) Computer Operations (i.e., mounting tapes, data batch processing, printer setup)

(B) Methodology Department (i.e., survey development, survey specifications, workflow process analysis)

(C) Human Resources Training Group (i.e., revision of training materials, updating training manuals)

(D) Computer Systems Analysis (i.e., customizing user computer systems, developing new systems applications)

Step 2. Scoring

Transfer your score for each item on the questionnaire to the scoring table. Calculate the average for each of the variables as indicated.

Step 3. Discussion

Meet in small groups to discuss and compare individual responses for each department.

QUESTIONNAIRE

The following questions pertain to the normal, usual, day-to-day pattern of work carried out by yourself and the people in your work unit. Please check the appropriate answers.

1. How many tasks are the same from day to day?

Very few of them			Some of them			Most of them
1	2	3	4	5	6	7

2. To what extent is there a clearly known way to do the major types of work you normally encounter?

To a small extent			To some extent			To a great extent
1	2	3	4	5	6	7

3. To what extent would you say your work is routine?

To a small extent			To some extent			To a great extent
1	2	3	4	5	6	7

4. To what extent is there a clearly defined body of knowledge of subject matter which can guide you in doing your work?

To a small extent			To some extent			To a great extent
1	2	3	4	5	6	7

5. To what extent is there an understandable sequence of steps that can be followed in doing your work?

To a small extent			To some extent			To a great extent
1	2	3	4	5	6	7

6. People in this unit do the same job in about the same way most of the time.

To a small extent		To some extent			To a great extent	
1	2	3	4	5	6	7

7. Basically, unit members perform repetitive activities in doing their jobs.

To a small extent		To some extent			To a great extent	
1	2	3	4	5	6	7

8. To do your work, to what extent can you actually rely on established procedures and practices?

To a small extent		To some extent			To a great extent	
1	2	3	4	5	6	7

9. How repetitious are your duties?

Very little		Moderate amount			Very much	
1	2	3	4	5	6	7

10. To what extent is there an understandable sequence of steps that can be followed in carrying out your work?

To a small extent		To some extent			To a great extent	
1	2	3	4	5	6	7

SCORING TABLE

Task Variability	Problem Analyzability
Item 1:	Item 2:
Item 3:	Item 4:
Item 6:	Item 5:
Item 7:	Item 8:
Item 9:	Item 10:
Total	Total
Divide by 5	Divide by 5
Average score:	Average score:

Exercise Feedback Form

Chapter 7—Exercise 19

Name: _____ **Student ID:** _____

1. What similarities/differences exist among the four departments in the exercise?

2. What special issues arise as a result of the levels of analyzability and variability present in a department? How might the structure be impacted?

3. What levels of analyzability and variability did you find for your department? Do the scores reflect your understanding of the structure used in your case?

You may be asked to complete and turn in this form to your instructor.

EXERCISE 20

Athletics and Physical Interdependence Technologies

I. Objective:

To explore differences in interdependence, coordination, and management between various athletic teams.

II. Process:

Step 1. Complete Chart

When the instructor indicates, complete the chart on page 108 comparing baseball, football, basketball and soccer teams.

Step 2. Discussion

When directed by your instructor, form groups to discuss the results.

	Baseball	Football	Basketball	Soccer
Interdependence (Pooled, Sequential or Reciprocal)				
Physical Dispersion of Players (High, Medium or Low)				
Coordination (Type of coordination)				
Key Management Job (Primary focus of management)				

Exercise Feedback Form

Chapter 7—Exercise 20

Name: _____ **Student ID:** _____

1. What similarities/differences exist among the four sports in the exercise?

2. What issues arise as a result of the level of interdependence in a department? How might the structure be impacted?

3. How might you assess other team sports (i.e., ice hockey, rugby, etc.) using this approach? Are there other sports that closely resemble those in the exercise in terms of interdependence?

You may be asked to complete and turn in this form to your instructor.

EXERCISE 21

The Hollow Square

I. Objectives:

To demonstrate problems in the relationship between those who design or create a plan and those who have the responsibility for executing it, to explore the implications of clear communication in a problem-solving task and to become aware of the factors that promote and inhibit effective problem solving.

II. Process:

Step 1. Group Formation

The class will be divided into one or more teams consisting of planners, operators, and observers. The triads of planner-operator-observer will be identified so people will know with whom they are working.

Step 2. Briefings

Report to the areas assigned by the instructor and read the appropriate briefing sheet for your group. The briefings are found at the end of the exercise.

Step 3. Planning and Instructing

The planners should proceed according to their instructions for the exact length of time stated by the instructor. The operators should work separately, according to their briefing sheet, until contacted by the planners. The observers should meet briefly to divide their responsibilities for observation; they will then take notes on the behavior of the planners and operators. Before the end of Step 3 the planners must call in their operators. The planners will spend at least 5 minutes briefing the operators.

Step 4. Assembly

The operators, working as teams and competing against one another, must assemble the hollow-square puzzle as quickly as possible. The team with the fastest assembly time will be declared the winner.

Step 5. Discussion

Planners: Select three adjectives to describe your feelings about the operators.

Operators: Select three adjectives to describe your feelings about planning before the planners called you in, and three about your feelings after they called you in.

Observers: Report your perceptions of the operators and planners before they interacted with each other.

Each operating team: Report on the instructions that you received from planners. How did this ultimately affect your ability to assemble the hollow square?

BRIEFING FOR PLANNING TEAM

Overview

Each of you will be given a packet containing several cardboard pieces that, when properly assembled, will make a hollow square design. During the assigned time you are to do the following:

1. Plan how the 17 pieces distributed among you should be assembled to make the design.

2. Instruct your operating team on how to implement your plan. You may begin instructing your operating team at any time during the planning period - but no later than 5 minutes before they are to begin the assembling process.

General Rules

1. You must keep all of the pieces you have in front of you at all times.

2. You may not touch the pieces held by other team members or trade pieces with other members of your team during the Planning and Instructing Phase.

3. You may not show the "Hollow Square Key" to the operating team at any time.

4. You may not assemble the entire square at any time (this is to be left to your operating team).

5. You are not to mark on any of the pieces.

6. Members of your operating team must also observe the above rules until the signal is given to begin assembling.

7. When time is called for your operating team to begin assembling the pieces, you may give no further instructions, but are to observe the operation.

BRIEFING FOR OPERATING TEAM

1. You will have responsibility for carrying out a task for four to six people, according to instructions given by your planning team. Your planning team may call you in to give you instructions at any time. If they do not summon you, you are to report to them when indicated by the instructor. You will be told when to begin your task; after that, no further instructions from your planning team can be given. You are to finish the assigned task as rapidly as possible.

2. While you are waiting for a call from your planning team, it is suggested that you discuss and make notes on the following:

   a. The feelings and concerns that you experience while waiting for instructions for the unknown task.

   b. Your suggestions on how a person might prepare to receive instructions.

3. Your notes recorded on the above will be helpful during the work group discussions following the completion of your task.

BRIEFING FOR OBSERVATION TEAM

Overview

You will be observing a situation in which a planning team decides how to solve a problem and gives instructions to an operating team for implementation. The problem consists of assembling 17 pieces of cardboard into the form of a hollow square. The planning team is supplied with the general layout of the pieces. The planning team is not to assemble the parts itself, but is to instruct the operating team on how to assemble the parts in a minimum amount of time. You will be silent observers throughout the process.

Some Suggestions for Observing

1. Each member of the observing team should watch the general pattern of communication but give special attention to one member of the planning team (during the planning phase) and one member of the operating team (during the assembly phase).

2. During the planning phase, watch for such behavior as

   a. The evenness or unevenness of participation among planning team members;

   b. Behavior that blocks or facilitates understanding;

   c. How the planning team divides its time between planning and instructing (how early does it invite the operating team to come in?);

   d. How well it plans its procedure for giving instructions to the operating team.

3. During the instructing phase (when the planning team is instructing the operating team), watch for such things as

   a. Who in the planning team gives the instructions (and how was this decided)?

   b. How is the operating team oriented to the task?

   c. What assumptions made by the planning team are not communicated to the operating team?

   d. How complete and clear are the instructions?

   e. How free does the operating team feel to ask questions of the planners?

4. During the assembly phase (when the operating team is working alone), watch for such things as

    a. Evidence that instructions were understood or misunderstood.

    b. Nonverbal reactions of planning team members as they watch their plans being implemented or distorted.

Exercise Feedback Form

Chapter 7—Exercise 21

Name: _____ **Student ID:** _____

1. What are some critical elements that a team of planners should consider when it is design-
    ing a task for others to carry out?

2. What can the operators do to help the work of the planners, and to insure that the task is
    completed accurately and rapidly?

3. In what departments, areas, or divisions of organizations are these problems most likely to
    occur? Why?

You may be asked to complete and turn in this form to your instructor.

Chapter 8

Information Technology and Control

EXERCISE 22

WACKKL

I. Objective:

To demonstrate that feedback plays a crucial role in strategic control systems that enable firms to evaluate their performance on a timely and accurate basis.

II. Process:

Step 1. Introduction

In this exercise you will be assigned a role which will require you to relay information about a product known as a Wackkl. As the exercise progresses, the amount and type of feedback will vary and this will influence the accuracy and timeliness of the information which is communicated. Strategic control in organizations refers to the overall evaluation of the company's performance. Feedback is a crucial element in the success of the strategic control system.

Step 2. Role Assignments

Your instructor will assign you to play one of three roles in Alphas Inc., a firm which designs, manufactures and sells state-of-the-art alphas; the exact nature of the alpha product will become clearer as the exercise develops. The personal names associated with the three roles are Sandy, Randi and Meryl.

Step 3. The Wackkl Scenario

Alphas, Inc. is a leading firm in the design, manufacturing and sales of state-of-the-art alphas. The product life cycle for alphas is approximately 15 months. At the end of the life cycle, the firm must be positioned to introduce its new model or lose significantly to competitors in this highly competitive industry. Through the years the physical shape of alphas has changed dramatically. Indeed, the industry depends on renewing consumer interest through the periodic introduction of exciting new models. Product design work is done by Sandy and manufacturing systems design is directed by Randi. The role of Meryl will be introduced later by your instructor.

It is now February 1, the beginning of the twelfth month in the life cycle of the firm's most popular alpha, the wackkl. Randi knows from past experience that it will take approximately 30 days to create a new manufacturing process for the new wackkl, another 30 days to produce the first batch of wackkls and a final 30 days to distribute the new wackkls to retail outlets. At the moment, however, Sandy is in Canada. To gather inspiration for the new wackkl design, Sandy has been examining traditional intercultural wackkls in the town of Waswanipi which has a population of approximately 1,200 people. Waswanipi is located in a very isolated region of northern Quebec. Sandy is staying at Wally's Western Waye Motel near the historic Waswanipi House on the shores of Lake Waswanipi from which the Waswanipi River rises and then flows through the Waswanipi valley.

Earlier today, Randi was relieved to receive a prototype of the new wackkl from Sandy via DHL. In order to minimize the size of the carton necessary to mail the wackkl, Sandi sent the wackkl in disassembled form; it has five pieces. Randi examines the five pieces and is not able to assemble them. Randi hopes that Sandy will call soon to explain how to assemble the pieces as every minute is now crucial for meeting the March 1 deadline.

An email is received, unexpectedly, from the Quebec Provincial Police with the message that Waswanipi has experienced a blizzard and is without electricity. It will be days before any traffic can get into or out of Waswanipi. In addition, the police email explains, Sandy's cell phone is partially broken—it can send but not receive voice transmissions. Sandy has no other means of sending or receiving messages. Randi is told that very soon Sandy will begin a series of cell phone calls with exact instructions about how to assemble the pieces of the Wackkl.

Step 4. Wackkl Assembly

Further instructions will come from your instructor.

Step 5. Discussion

Specific discussion instructions will be provided by your instructor.

Exercise Feedback Form

Chapter 8—Exercise 22

Name: _____   **Student ID:** _____

1. What difficulties were experienced by Sandy in the initial attempt to give instructions to Randi about how to assemble the wackkl?

2. What difficulties were experienced by Randi in the initial attempt to follow instructions given by Sandy about how to assemble the wackkl?

3. Was it easier to assemble the wackkl after the lightning strike? Why or why not?

You may be asked to complete and turn in this form to your instructor.

EXERCISE 23

The Balanced Scorecard

I. Objective:

To reinforce the general concept of the balanced scorecard approach and to familiarize students with the four scorecard zones of finance, customers, processes and learning/growth.

II. Process:

Step 1. Introduction.

In this exercise you are provided with two lists: (1) eight company objectives; (2) eight measures. The activity of the exercise consists of matching the objectives with measures and then classifying the matched objectives and measures into the four basic scorecard zones of finance, customers, processes and learning/growth.

Step 2. Match company objectives with measurements.

Match the objectives in the Table 1 below with the measures in Table 2 and record your matches (numbers and letters only) in Table 3.

Table 1. Objectives
1. To be the cost leader in our market by 2007
2. To reduce customer return by 75% within 12 months
3. To lead the market in speedy delivery by 2011
4. To build a sports and social club by March 2012
5. To increase profitability by 20% by 2008
6. To produce products that are right first time within 3 months
7. To train and develop all team leaders by 2009
8. To achieve 99% customer satisfaction within 5 years

Table 2. Measures

(a) Average time taken for customers to receive complete orders

(b) Customer retention rates

(c) Return On Capital Employed (ROCE)

(d) Employee satisfaction rates

(e) Statistical process control

(f) Employee retention rates

(g) Customer feedback or complaints

(h) Unit cost

Table 3. Matched Objectives and Measures

Objectives	Measures
1.	2.
3.	4.
5.	6.
7.	8.

Step 3. Classify objectives.

Classify the matched objectives and measurements in one of the four scorecard zones in Table 4.

Table 4. Scorecard Zones
1. Finance

Objectives	Measures

| 2. Customer ||
Objectives	Measures

| 3. Business Processes ||
Objectives	Measures

| 4. Learning and Growth ||
Objectives	Measures

Step 4. Discussion

Specific discussion instructions will be provided by your instructor.

Exercise Feedback Form

Chapter 8—Exercise 23

Name: _____ **Student ID:** _____

1. What negative outcomes might result from a much greater emphasis being given to business processes than the other three scorecard zones? Why

2. Imagine that you are the owner and principal manager of a small independent doughnut baking and retail sales business. In your opinion, which one of the four scorecard zones would be most difficult for you to keep in balance with the other three zones? Why?

3. Use your imagination to develop a third objective for the business process zone. What would you use as a measure for this additional business process objective? Why?

You may be asked to complete and turn in this form to your instructor.

EXERCISE 24

Effective Organizational Control Mechanisms?

I. Objective:

To explore the various considerations of implementing an effective organizational control mechanism and to identify specific criteria that can be used to evaluate the appropriateness of control mechanisms.

II. Process:

Step 1. The Control Mechanism

Your instructor has decided to add to your educational experience by inviting a local business leader to address your class. Aware that your university has a strict parking policy that includes rigorous enforcement of violations ($25.00 fine), your instructor has decided to request a waiver of the daily parking fee ($1.00) for this important guest. Upon further examination, your instructor discovers that the university has developed a control procedure to preclude abuse of the parking fee waiver that includes the completion of a "Request for Complimentary Parking Permits" form.

Step 2. Parking Fee Waiver Form

Review the form on the next page and answer the following question: "What's wrong with this control mechanism?"

REQUEST FOR COMPLIMENTARY PARKING PERMITS

Please provide the information requested below and forward. If you wish to provide a list of persons attending please attach. If you have any question contact J. Smith, ext. 1111.

REQUESTING DEPARTMENT: _____

PERSON REQUESTING: _____

PHONE: _____

EVENT: _____

DATE(S): _____

TIME(S): _____

NUMBER OF PERSONS FOR EVENT: _____

PERMITS MAILED OR ISSUED AT INFORMATION BOOTH: _____

JUSTIFICATION FOR WAIVED FEES: _____

_____

_____

_____

APPROVAL/DISAPPROVAL SIGNATURES

Dean: _____Date: _____

Approve: _____   Disapprove: _____

Vice President: _____Date: _____

Approve: _____   Disapprove: _____

Exercise Feedback Form

Chapter 8—Exercise 24

Name: _____ **Student ID:** _____

1. Is the control cost-effective?

2. Is the control acceptable? Appropriate?

3. Is the process strategic? Reliable and objective?

You may be asked to complete and turn in this form to your instructor.

Chapter 9

Organization Size, Life Cycle, and Decline

EXERCISE 25

Discovering an Organization's Life Cycle

I. Objectives:

To acquire experience in obtaining organizational information from electronic or traditional documentary sources, to become familiar with the organizational development of an actual firm and to develop an understanding of four stages in the life cycle of organizations.

II. Process:

Step 1. Company Selection

This exercise may be accomplished individually or in groups but, either way, the initial step is to select a business firm. Among the possible sources of firms for this exercise are the various lists of companies maintained by Fortune, Inc., such as The Fortune 500, The Fortune 1000, The Fortune 100 Fastest Growing Firms and the Fortune Global 500. Your instructor may provide you with an alternate list or a specific company.

Step 2. Research

As directed by your instructor, obtain detailed current and historical information about your assigned firm. Sources of such information are found in library collections of company annual reports, various directories of firms including the series maintained by Dun and Bradstreet, Inc., and the World Wide Web. One possible starting place on the World Wide Web is the Hoover's online link which can be found on Fortune's home page (www.fortune.com).

Step 3. Analysis

Study the four categories shown on p. 136 and, within the time allotted by your instructor, determine (1) the current life cycle stage of your assigned firm by documenting as many of the characteristics listed on p. 136 as time will permit and (2) the approximate time periods when your assigned firm was at the other stages. In most cases, the classification of a firm will not be uniform. For example, a company may be at the elaboration level in terms of structure and top management style but still at the formalization stage in terms of the other characteristics. Thus, the best strategy is to strive to determine, *in general*, which stage the company seems to be operating in and the time periods of other stages.

Step 4. Report

Describe, for the rest of the class, your assigned firm and your conclusions in terms of the current life cycle of the company and approximate time periods when the company was at other stages.

Characteristics of Four Life Cycle Stages*

Characteristics of Four Life Cycle Stages	ENTREPRENEURIAL	COLLECTIVITY	FORMALIZATION	ELABORATION
General Description	Infancy; new and small; energy is devoted to survival	Youth; rapid growth; excited commitment to the firm's mission	Midlife; internal stability and market expansion; delegation with formal systems	Maturity; complete organization with teams; focus on firm's status
Major Crisis of the Stage	Need for leadership	Need for delegation	Too much red tape	Need for revitalization
Extent of Bureaucracy	Nonbureaucratic	Prebureaucratic	Bureaucratic	Very Bureaucratic
Structure	Informal; one-person show	Informal with a few procedures	Formal procedures; division of labor; new specialties	Teamwork within bureaucracy; small-company thinking
Products or services	Single product or service	Major product or service, with variations	Complete line of products or services	Multiple product or service lines
Reward/control systems	Personal/paternalistic	Personal/ contribution to success	Impersonal/ formalized systems	Extensive/ tailored to product and department
Innovation	By owner-manager	By employees and managers	By separate innovation group	By R&D department
Goal	Survival	Growth	Stability and expansion	Reputation and completeness
Top management Style	Individualistic and entrepreneurial	Charismatic and direction-giving	Delegation with controls	Teamwork and attack bureaucracy

*(Adapted from Richard Daft, *Organization Theory and Design*, Thomson Learning, 2006)

Exercise Feedback Form

Chapter 9—Exercise 25

Name: _____   **Student ID:** _____

1. What is the name of the firm which you studied for this exercise? What sources of information did you use to document life cycle stages of this firm?

2. What difficulties did you encounter in collecting information for this exercise and performing the analysis?

3. What are the approximate time periods of the four stages of your firm?

You may be asked to complete and turn in this form to your instructor.

EXERCISE 26

How Big Are the Colleges?

I. Objective:

To examine the various definitions of organizational size.

II. Process

Step 1: Compare Colleges

Review the comparison chart (p. 140) of various college characteristics.

Step 2: Rank Colleges

Based upon the statistics provided on p. 140, rank order the four colleges in terms of size beginning with the biggest college ranked as number one.

Step 3: Group Ranking

Compare your ranks with those of other class members. Attempt to reconcile differences and arrive at a group consensus.

Comparison of Characteristics of Colleges

	College A	College B	College C	College D	"Your College"
Total Enrollment	33,327	13,715	43,382	10,634	
Undergraduate Enrollment	26,075	8,628	31,633	7,994	
Land Area	463 a	260 a	2,000 a	1,250 a	
Funded Endowments	$286 M	$465 M	$681 M	$3,100 M	
Total Faculty	1,897	1,122	1,809	1,057	
Full-Time Faculty	1,017	774	1,745	726	
Part-Time Faculty	880	348	54	331	
Total Freshmen	5,153	1,859	3,705	1,971	
Acceptance Percentage	54%	53%	62%	34%	
Freshman National Merit Scholars	39	12	166	45	
Library Volumes	2,310,597	2,000,000	3,401,279	2,704,394	
Library Periodicals	15,228	19,551	25,213	24,334	
Library Materials Expenditures	$5.2 M	$1.8 M	$8.7 M	$6.8 M	
Computers	233	2,000	604	880	
Housing Spaces	4,815	3,793	6,779	6,242	

Exercise Feedback Form

Chapter 9—Exercise 26

Name: _____   **Student ID:** _____

1. What ranks did you assign to the four colleges?

2. What criterion did you use to assign ranks to the colleges? Why?

3. Develop a composite index of weighted criteria using at least five of the statistics presented. How do the colleges rank when this index is used?

You may be asked to complete and turn in this form to your instructor.

EXERCISE 27

Bureaucracy and You?

I. Objectives:

Two related purposes are intended to be served by this exercise. Since all people seek some degree of order in their lives, the bureaucratic form of organization appeals to all people, but **in varying degrees** hence one purpose of the exercise is to provide students with the opportunity to assess their own orientation to bureaucracy. A second purpose of the exercise is to provide students with the opportunity to assess their own major field of study in terms of orientation toward bureaucracy. Hopefully, these two purposes will serve a larger concern which is to enable all to develop a broad point of view as to the usefulness of a given organization system.

II. Process:

Step 1. Introduction

A person with a bureaucratic orientation is one who fits comfortably into the role of working in a bureaucracy. Unless the world were populated with people who adjust readily to working for a bureaucracy, organizations such as AT&T or the Ford Motor Co. could not function. Other people—those with a low bureaucratic orientation—experience feelings of discomfort working for a bureaucracy. The bureaucratic orientation scale presented next gives you a chance to acquire tentative (not scientifically proved) information about your position on this important aspect of work life.

Step 2. Complete Test—Determine Score

Although the bureaucratic orientation scale is a self-examination and research tool, a very high score (15 or over) would suggest that you would enjoy working in a bureaucracy. A very low score (5 or lower) would suggest that you would be frustrated by working in a bureaucracy, especially a large one.

Step 3. Discussion

Your instructor will provide discussion points.

Exercise Feedback Form

Chapter 9—Exercise 27

Name: _____ **Student ID:** _____

1. Do you think your score is representative of most college students in your major?

2. Of most students at this university?

3. Of most people who graduated from high school during the 2-3 year period when you did?

4. What are the implications, if any, regarding organizational structure?

You may be asked to complete and turn in this form to your instructor.

The Bureaucratic Orientation "Test"

Answer each question "mostly agree" or "mostly disagree." Assume that you are trying to learn something about yourself. Do not assume that your answer will be shown to a prospective employer or, for that matter, anyone else.

MOSTLY AGREE	MOSTLY DISAGREE	
_____	_____	1. I value stability in my job.
_____	_____	2. I like a predictable organization.
_____	_____	3. The best job for me would be one in which the future is uncertain.
_____	_____	4. The military would be a nice place to work.
_____	_____	5. Rules, policies and procedures tend to frustrate me.
_____	_____	6. I would enjoy working for a company that employed 85,000 people worldwide.
_____	_____	7. Being self-employed would involve more risk than I am willing to take.
_____	_____	8. Before accepting a job, I would like to see an exact job description.
_____	_____	9. I would prefer a job as a freelance house painter to one as a clerk for the Department of Motor Vehicles.
_____	_____	10. Seniority should be as important as performance in determining pay increases and promotion.
_____	_____	11. It would give me a feeling of pride to work for the largest and most successful company in its field.
_____	_____	12. Given a choice, I would prefer to make $70,000 per year as a vice president in a small company to $80,000 as a staff specialist in a large company.
_____	_____	13. I would regard wearing an employee badge with a number on it as a degrading experience.
_____	_____	14. Parking spaces in a company lot should be assigned on the basis of job level.
_____	_____	15. I would generally prefer working as a specialist to wearing many hats.

_____ _____ 16. Before accepting a job (given a choice), I would want to make sure that the company had a good program of employee benefits.

_____ _____ 17. A company will probably not be successful unless it establishes a clear set of rules and regulations.

_____ _____ 18. Regular working hours and vacations are more important to me than finding thrills on the job.

_____ _____ 19. You should respect people according to their rank.

_____ _____ 20. Rules are meant to be broken.

Scoring

Give yourself a plus one for each question that you answered in the bureaucratic direction:

1. Mostly agree	8. Mostly agree	15. Mostly disagree
2. Mostly agree	9. Mostly disagree	16. Mostly agree
3. Mostly disagree	10. Mostly agree	17. Mostly agree
4. Mostly agree	11. Mostly agree	18. Mostly agree
5. Mostly disagree	12. Mostly disagree	19. Mostly agree
6. Mostly agree	13. Mostly disagree	20. Mostly disagree
7. Mostly agree	14. Mostly agree	

Chapter 10

Organizational Culture and Ethical Values

EXERCISE 28

My Friend Morgan

I. Objective:

To help students recognize opinions about ethical behavior, provide an opportunity for discussing relationships between personal behavior and professional responsibility, and provide a vehicle for discussing theories of ethical behavior.

II. Process:

Step 1. Survey

Complete the survey which appears on p. 151.

Step 2. My Friend Morgan

Read the scenario provided by your instructor. Be prepared to discuss.

My Friend Morgan

Use a checkmark to indicate a yes or true answer and leave the line blank to signify a no or false answer.

During your lifetime, have you ever:	In the past year, have you:	
_____	_____	Stolen something from work, a friend, a family member, etc.?
_____	_____	Shoplifted?
_____	_____	Lied or not told the truth?
_____	_____	Cheated on your spouse or significant other?
_____	_____	Kept merchandise or money when the sales clerk or company made a mistake in your favor?
_____	_____	Lied on an employment application?
_____	_____	Used illegal drugs?
_____	_____	Cheated on a test or exam?
_____	_____	Broken the law or committed a crime not already mentioned in this survey (excluding speeding)?
_____	_____	Plagiarized another person's work?
_____	_____	Compromised your personal ethics to do something required for your job?
_____	_____	Switched the price tag on merchandise?
_____	_____	Knowingly bought merchandise (perhaps for a special event or occasion), used it, then returned it?
_____	_____	Unhooked or tampered with the car's odometer?
_____	_____	Falsified work-related expense, travel, or time records?
_____	_____	Charged personal items to the company (copies, etc.) and didn't pay for them?
_____	_____	Falsified a subordinate's performance evaluation?

Exercise Feedback Form

Chapter 10—Exercise 28

Name: _____ **Student ID:** _____

1. Does a company have the right to be interested in employees' off-work behavior? At what point does personal life spill over into work life?

2. Would the type of job make a difference in your recommendation (i.e., an international assignment)?

3. Would you or would you not recommend Morgan? Why?

You may be asked to complete and turn in this form to your instructor.

EXERCISE 29

Culture in the Land of Doone

I. Objectives:

To enhance participants' understanding of the interpersonal and organizational effects of culture shock, to learn about unfamiliar cultures and why training techniques must fit trainees' cultures.

II. Process:

Step 1. Introduction

Critter Technologies was founded by Ima Critter, a genetic engineer and an entrepreneur. He believes that there is a significant market for Critters—furry, rodent-like organisms with six legs. The company uses genetic engineering technologies to manufacture Critters. The purpose they serve is a trade secret. A group of inventors recently created an improved critter called Critter B, and they hope to sell it to Critter Technologies. The inventors believe that the best way to demonstrate its superiority is to train the company's executives to assemble the prototype. For this purpose, Mr. Critter invited them to visit his facilities in Doone, a unique community located in a remote area of the United States.

Step 2. Preparation

Inventors: Study the prototype of Critter B, determine how you will train the executives to assemble it, and prepare to do so. The executives must be able to assemble the prototype to understand why it is superior to existing Critters. As such, this is the goal of the program.

Executives and observers: Study the information provided by the instructor.

Step 3. Orientation

One inventor visits Doone (the room in which the executives and observers are preparing). He or she meets the executives, describes the upcoming training program, and answers their questions. After visiting for a brief time, the inventor returns to his or her group to finalize preparations.

EXERCISE 30

A Culture in the Forest

I. Objective:

To become familiar with the basic components of organizational culture by considering an unusual "nonprofit" organizational setting.

II. Process:

Step 1. Introduction

When assigned by the instructor, read the following case of an organization which is widely known although not exactly well documented!

THE ENTREPRENEUR

Robin Hood awoke just as the sun was creeping over the crest of the hill in the very middle of Sherwood Forest. He was not the least rested, for he had not slept well that night. He could not get to sleep because of all the problems he was going to have to face today.

Certainly his campaign against the sheriff was going well, perhaps too well. It had all started out as a personal quarrel between the two of them, but now it was much more than just that. There was a price on his head of 1000 pounds, and there was no doubt that he was causing the sheriff a great deal of trouble, as taxes went uncollected or unde-livered to the Crown, and rich men could not sleep soundly at night anywhere near Sherwood.

Things had changed since the early days, however. In those days it was just a small band of men, united in their cause against the sheriff, and for that matter, against Prince John, for the sheriff was simply doing John's bidding. But that was no longer the case. The fame of the Merry Men had grown and with it their numbers. He used to know each man as both a friend and companion, but now he didn't even know all of their names. Little John continued to keep discipline among the men as well as maintaining their skills with the bow, while Will Scarlet kept an eye on the sheriff, as well as any rich prospect who was foolish enough to travel Sherwood. Scarlock took care of the loot as he always had, and Much the Miller's Son continued to keep the men fed.

All this success was leading to problems. Game was, frankly, getting scarce as the num-ber of men in the band increased, and the corresponding demand for food grew. Likely targets for the Merry Men were getting to hard find as more and more wealthy travelers were giving Sherwood a wide berth, reluctant as they were to part with their gold. Finally, the Sheriff and his men were getting better. Robin had always had the advantage of knowing Sherwood better than any man alive, but now there were at least several men who knew it almost as well as he, and some of them wore the colors of Prince John.

All this was leading Robin to reconsider his old ways. Perhaps a simple transit tax through Sherwood might be a part of the answer. But a tax might destroy his support among the people of the forest, and it had been rejected by the Merry Men, who were proud of their motto "Rob from the rich and give to the poor!" Besides, he needed the support of the poor, as they were his main source of information on the movements of the sheriff.

Killing the sheriff was not the answer. He would just be replaced, and aside from quenching Robin's personal thirst for revenge, the new sheriff might be even more treacherous. Robin hated his enemy, but he had the advantage of knowing the sheriff's strengths and weaknesses. He would not know a new man's talents.

Prince John, on the other hand, was a vicious tyrant; a good part of his tyranny stemmed from his very weakness. The Barons were growing more restless every day, and the people simply hated him. They wanted King Richard back from his jail in Austria. Robin had been discreetly approached by several nobles loyal to Richard to join in the effort to free the King with the promise of a full pardon for him and all his men should they succeed. But Robin knew that if they failed, John would burn Sherwood and the rest of England to the ground to reap his vengeance. Theft and unrest in the provinces was one thing, intrigue at court was another.

Robin knew the days of the Merry Men were numbered. Even as they grew stronger, they grew weaker. Time was on the side of the sheriff, who could draw on all the power of the Crown if he had to, and, if Robin became too much of a threat, would surely do so.

Just then the horn blew for the traditional English breakfast of bread and ale. Robin would have breakfast with the Merry Men and then confer with Will Scarlet, Little John, and Scarlock.

Step 2. Discussion

Discuss the following questions in small groups, or consider them individually, and be prepared to discuss your answers with the class.

1. What are the central values of this culture and what rituals, would you imagine, help to reinforce these values?

2. Who is the hero of the culture of this organization and what networks would be able to support the hero's status?

3. How strong is this culture? It the culture a dominant feature of the organization as reported? Is the culture "lived by top management"?

4. It would seem as if organizational size has become a major factor in the problems considered by Hood. How has organizational size affected the nature of this organization's culture?

5. Given the issues which Hood is pondering, do you envision any changes in the Band's culture in the near future? Why or Why not? If changes are envisioned, what might they be?

Exercise Feedback Form

Chapter 10—Exercise 30

Name: _____ **Student ID:** _____

1. What are some of the situations in the environment that will have an impact on whatever Robin decides to do?

2. What are some of the alternatives that Robin is considering for dealing with his problems? Can you identify some additional alternatives?

3. What do you think Robin should do?

You may be asked to complete and turn in this form to your instructor.

Chapter 11

Innovation and Change

EXERCISE 31

Dynamics of Change

I. Objective:

To demonstrate the various forms of resistance to change that may occur in an organizational setting.

II. Process:

Step 1. Introduction

Your instructor will provide additional information for you to respond to, both individually and in small groups.

Step 2. Classification

Classify the resultant responses to the instructor-provided information using the following list:

1. Excessive focus on costs. The mind-set that costs are all-important and that other elements, such as changes to increase employee motivation or customer satisfaction, are unimportant

2. Failure to perceive benefits. Any significant change will produce both positive and negative reactions. If the organization's reward system discourages risk-taking, a change process may falter because employees think that the risk of making the change is too high.

3. Lack of coordination and cooperation. Organizational fragmentation and conflict often result from the lack of coordination for change implementation. Moreover, in the case of new technology, the old and new systems may not be compatible.

4. Uncertainty avoidance. At the individual level, many employees fear the uncertainty associated with change and will attempt to ignore the change.

5. Fear of loss. Managers and employees may fear the loss of power and status or even their jobs.

Step 3. Discussion

Discuss the implications of varied degrees of resistance to change for the organization in small groups. Address specific techniques that may be useful in reducing the impact of resistance to change.

Exercise Feedback Form

Chapter 11—Exercise 31

Name: _____   **Student ID:** _____

1. How did you feel after the instructor revealed the purpose of the exercise? Why? Which one of the five barriers to change did you personally experience most strongly?

2. Which one of the five barriers do you believe would be most prominent in a small, entrepreneurial, software development company where most employees perform non-routine tasks using specialized skills? Why?

3. Which one of the five barriers do you believe would be most prominent in a large, bureaucratic, labor-intensive, manufacturing company where most employees perform routine tasks using non-specialized skills? Why?

You may be asked to complete and turn in this form to your instructor.

EXERCISE 32

Change Requires "Intensive Care!"

I. Objectives:

As a result of participating in this exercise, students should be able to (a) identify reactions to change efforts, (b) experience the emotions surrounding change, (c) identify how different stakeholders interpret change, (d) describe the role of information processing in the change process, and (e) describe how organizational justice issues influence the change process.

II. Process:

Step 1. Introduction

The exercise engages students in analyzing a change, making decisions based on the change, and communicating information regarding the change as either a member of the management team or the employee team. The activity explores issues such as organizational justice, survivor reactions, psychological contracts, communication, and leadership.

Step 2. St. Mary's Hospital scenario

Read the case background titled "St. Mary's Hospital" in Appendix A.

Step 3. Employment

You are employed by St. Mary's and will be provided with a number of memos, press releases, and so on, to react and respond to throughout the course of the exercise.

Step 4. Assignment of role

You will be assigned a role and a management team or employee team based on your assigned job role.

Step 5. Join Management or Employee Team

Rearrange your seats so that you are a member of either the management team or the employee team.

Step 6. Press release

Read the press release. Both teams should brainstorm the following question: As a stakeholder, what do you want to know?

Step 7. Scenario

From this point on, a number of memos, press releases and other information will be provided to each team. The teams will be asked to formulate responses/reactions at various points. Be sure to record your responses for further discussion.

Step 8. Discussion

Your instructor will facilitate a discussion at the conclusion of the exercise. You may be asked to report your particular viewpoint based on your role or that of the team to which you were assigned.

Exercise Feedback Form

Chapter 11—Exercise 32

Name: _____ Student ID: _____

1. How did you feel during the activity?

2. How did you feel about the meeting with your supervisor/employees? What occurred during this meeting?

3. What were the underlying themes regarding change that were reinforced through this exercise?

4. What should have been done differently?

You may be asked to complete and turn in this form to your instructor.

Appendix A

St. Mary's Hospital

You are employed by St. Mary's Hospital, which is located in Bay Run, a large Midwestern city (population 700,000). St. Mary's is an inner-city Catholic hospital that was started in the early 1900s by a local Catholic Church. It has retained its religious affiliation through the years, even though many such hospitals have been acquired by for-profit health care conglomerates. Over the years, as many city residents have migrated to the suburbs, St. Mary's has found itself increasingly serving the indigent population. At the same time, health care has undergone tremendous changes; costs have skyrocketed, insurance companies have dictated the type of care and length of stay in the hospital, and alternative delivery methods of health care have decreased the need for many people to use hospitals. These changes have profoundly affected St. Mary's. For example, in 1983, St. Mary's was a 650-bed hospital. In 1996, there are 280 beds in the hospital. To accommodate these changes, St. Mary's has gone through several staff-reduction phases. Although these reductions have been difficult, the staff at St. Mary's remains very dedicated to its mission of providing quality health care to anyone who comes through its doors.

A lot of this staff dedication can be attributed to the strong leadership of its president, Marilyn Smithers. Ms. Smithers has been in various administrative positions at St. Mary's for 18 years. She has been president for the past 10 years. Under her direction, staff and service reductions have been made. Ms. Smithers has always been a hands-on administrator. When staff cuts were made, she visited every department and explained why and how the cuts were made. She is frequently seen wandering the halls, visiting both employees and patients. She knows practically all 1,000 employees by name.

St. Mary's is the smallest of four hospitals in Bay Run. South Side has approximately 500 beds, and Riverview is a 600-bed hospital serving primarily the north side of the city. The largest of the four hospitals is University, which is a 900-bed teaching hospital located in University Heights, a suburb on the west side of town.

Many believe Bay Run no longer needs four hospitals with all the emergicenters and long-term health care facilities being built. For about a year, there have been rumors that St. Mary's will be the first hospital to go.

EXERCISE 33

Environment, Power, and Change

I. Objectives:

To describe the exchanges influencing power differentials in organizations, to understand the four environmental change drivers and to analyze how change drivers impact ideas and needs and the adoption of change.

II. Process:

Step 1. Review Organizational Change Drivers

The overall theoretical perspective of this exercise is that certain "drivers" directly affect (1) *ideas* and (2) *needs* as well as success of organizations (3) *adoption* of changes by increasing organizational member power. These drivers are shown in the table on p. 175.

Step 2. Golf Cart Inc., Five Scenarios

Your organization manufactures golf carts and sells them to country clubs, golf courses, and consumers. Your group is faced with the task of assessing how environmental changes will affect individuals' organizational power. As assigned by your instructor, read each scenario and then identify the five members in the organization (see box on p. 175) whose power will increase most in light of the following environmental conditions:

1. New computer-aided manufacturing technologies are being introduced in the workplace during the upcoming 2 to 18 months.

2. New federal emissions standards are being legislated by the government.

3. Sales are down significantly; the industry appears to be shrinking!

4. The company is planning to go international in the next 12 to 18 months.

5. The Equal Employment Opportunity Commission is applying pressure to balance the male-female population in the organization's upper hierarchy by threatening to publicize the predominance of men in upper management.

Step 3. Group Conclusions

As assigned by your instructor, meet with other members of your group and make a final determination of the five persons whose power would increase most in each of the scenarios.

Environmental Change Drivers	
Type of Driver	**Source of Change Drivers**
Social	Issues such as gender, race, age, diversity, or work-family conflict
Political	Pressures to manage public appearance and legal considerations
Economic	Financial pressures on a firm
Technological	Innovations and technological improvements necessary to compete

Fifteen Jobs in the Scenario Organizations

Advertising expert (male)	Accountant-CPA (male)	Product designer (male)
Chief financial officer (female)	General Manager (male)	In-house counsel (male)
Securities analyst (male)	Marketing manager (female)	Public relations expert (male)
Operations manager (female)	Computer designer (female)	HR manager (female)
Corporate trainer (male)	Industrial engineer (male)	Chemist (male)

Exercise Feedback Form

Chapter 11—Exercise 33

Name: _____ **Student ID:**_____

1. For each scenario, describe which change driver seems to be affecting the organization.

2. Which organization members did your group select for each scenario? Why?

3. In what way would the selected persons have had an influence on ideas, needs and the rate of adoption of change in the scenario organizations?

You may be asked to complete and turn in this form to your instructor.

Chapter 12

Decision-Making Processes

EXERCISE 34

Maximizing or Satisficing: Pick the Best—Or the First Good One!

I. Objective:

To explore alternative decision-making approaches.

II. Process:

Step 1. Computer Purchase

When told to do so, read the following situational description and place yourself in the role of Connie Heerman, a staff assistant to Betty Ewing, president of Ewing Manufacturing, which is a rapidly growing, medium-sized manufacturer of commercial air-conditioning equipment.

Situational description—Part A

Ewing Manufacturing has decided to discontinue its practice of contracting out its computer and data processing work. Betty Ewing, the president, has decided to purchase a computer system. As staff assistant to the president, you have been charged with evaluating the various systems and making a recommendation as to what computer should be purchased. Ewing's computer needs are very specialized. Regular equipment will not work. The regular computer manufacturers produce these special computers infrequently and the demand is very high. It is a seller's market.

You have contacted eight computer manufacturers and given all of them identical specifications. You find out that these manufacturers will call you when a machine becomes available. Each will quote you a price for a unit that will precisely meet your needs, but these quotes will come in one at a time. You have made some estimates and believe that $500,000, plus or minus $20,000, will be the cost.

Several suppliers have informed you that they may call you within the next three weeks with a price. You will be given a one-time price and you will have 48 hours to accept or reject the offer. If you reject the offer, the computer manufacturer will sell the equipment to another customer. If you accept it, you will receive no other offers. If you reject an offer, you may get some additional ones, but you do not know how many quotes you will receive! Since you must have this equipment you will have to take the last offer regardless of price, if you did not agree earlier to purchase one of the units.

You will now start receiving the bids. After each bid is made, place the name of the company and the price in the appropriate column of the Part I form. Then decide whether or not you accept the offer. Write your acceptance or rejection in the column on the right. Remember the proposals come several days apart and when you turn one down (with the exception of the last one), it will be rescinded.

Step 2. Printer Purchase

Situation description—Part B

Now that you have the computer, you become aware of several new applications for Ewing Manufacturing. With the addition of an on-line, high-speed printer, you estimate you can significantly improve productivity.

There are several units which seem to meet your needs, according to your research. Most of them have the capability to produce at the level which you want. However, there are some differences with respect to durability and maintenance. When you ask the manufacturers for bids, you receive them from only three of the firms.

They bids from each manufacturer are identical. There are some differences among machines with respect to the cost and frequency of repair.

The printers from which you can choose are listed below, with a brief rating of their maintenance records:

Acme Printer	This unit has acceptable performance capability. It has a rating of .25, which is the probability that it will experience a major breakdown within the next three years.
Brilliant Writer	This unit is equally adequate. Its maintenance rating is .20, the probability of a major breakdown within three years.
Clear Writer	This has the same performance capacity as the Acme and the Brilliant—the three-year maintenance rating is .10. Of all the machines it is the most dependable.

Step 3. Part II

When asked by your instructor, fill in the Part II form.

Part I

	Company	Offer	Accept or Reject
1.			
2.			
3.			
4.			
5.			
6.			
7.			
8.			

Part II

1. What other information do you need to make a good choice? _____

_____

_____

_____

_____

Basic Cost of Printer:

Acme Printer   _____

Brilliant Writer   _____

Clear Writer   _____

Compute expected cost of breakdown

Printer	Breakdown Cost		Probability of Breakdown		Expected Cost of Breakdown
Acme Printer	_____	*	_____	=	_____
Brilliant Writer	_____	*	_____	=	_____
Clear Writer	_____	*	_____	=	_____

Total cost computation (transfer the appropriate figures above to the table below)

Printer	Basic Cost		Expected Breakdown Cost		Total Cost
Acme Printer	_____	*	_____	=	_____
Brilliant Writer	_____	*	_____	=	_____
Clear Writer	_____	*	_____	=	_____

Which one is best? _____

2. Are there any circumstances under which you might purchase the Clear Writer, regardless of cost?   ☐ Yes ☐ No

What are they? _____

Exercise Feedback Form

Chapter 12—Exercise 34

Name: _____ **Student ID:** _____

1. If you selected the first computer offered, what reasons can you give for doing so?

2. Did the people who selected the last computer offered make an irrational decision?

3. Do organizations always make rational decisions? Satisficing decisions? Discuss.

You may be asked to complete and turn in this form to your instructor.

EXERCISE 35

Decisive Decision Making

I. Purpose:

To understand ethical frameworks and different perspectives, and to recognize the value of frameworks in decision making while raising awareness of one's own ethical agendas.

II. Process:

Step 1. Read the exercise.

You are the chief seismologist at one of the leading research facilities in North America. You hold a Ph.D. from the most prestigious university in the country specializing in this field. For a number of years, you have been working on perfecting a method for predicting major earthquakes on the West Coast. You report to the director of the research center. The organization is dependent on government agency funds in the form of research grants along with funding from corporate interests.

Recently, you have developed a sophisticated technique that you believe is able to forecast, within 80%, the likelihood of the occurrence of an earthquake during a 48-hour period. The results of a rigorous study that you have just completed indicate that a 7.3-magnitude quake will hit one of four fault lines in Southern California within the next 2 days. Three of the faults are in less populated areas where major damage will be relatively low. However, the fourth fault is the San Andreas, which, if affected, would result in significant damage to structures and a considerable number of casualties.

Step 2. Rank order choices.

Listed below are five alternative strategies. Indicate the action you would take by selecting the most appropriate item, and then rank order the remaining choices.

_____ Without discussing your findings, ask colleagues in your field what they would do "hypothetically" in a similar situation. Seek the advice of experts like yourself to confirm your decision; avoid actions that are not supported by your peers.

_____ You must share the information with the media. After informing the research director, it is your responsibility to make sure the news of this potential disaster is released to the public. Notifying the director and other government officials is not sufficient; important information may be withheld. You must be sure the truth is known.

_____ Refer to the procedures and policies manual published by the research institution. If the organization has a policy regarding the responsibility for the disclosure of information, you should follow these procedures.

_____ You must be very careful about the dissemination of your research findings. There is a 20% probability that the quake will not occur, and even if the quake does occur sharing information could be harmful. You will likely be held responsible for the chaos and panic that may result. Your career is at stake; you cannot afford to be wrong.

_____ You need to calculate the expected costs associated with the quake. That is, you must compare the value of sharing the information openly to that of maintaining silence. Given the probability of the occurrence of the quake, assign estimated values for injuries sustained, resources needed for cleanup, buildings/structures destroyed, and loss of life. Compare these calculations to estimated value related to releasing information. The amount should include an assessment of the reduction of injuries and deaths but should be offset by the costs of preparation and the pandemonium that is likely to result if prior information is known. (Assume you have a computer program that contains the financial estimates; you need only to enter probability.) If releasing information to the public has a higher expected value than remaining silent, then you must divulge your data.

Step 3. Group Discussion

Form groups of four to five students each. Discuss the issues and reach a group consensus, if possible. That is, try to find agreement regarding the rank order of the five choices.

Step 4. Class Discussion.

Interact with other groups regarding choices.

Discussion should focus on explaining reasons for selections.

Exercise Feedback Form

Chapter 12—Exercise 35

Name: _____ **Student ID:** _____

1. What was your personal first-choice decision? Why?

2. Was your personal first choice consistent with the choices of your group members?

3. Was an observable pattern of choice present in the class? What factor(s) might account for this outcome?

You may be asked to complete and turn in this form to your instructor.

EXERCISE 36

Winter Survival Exercise

I. Objectives:

To compare the effectiveness of several different methods of making decisions and to assess the advantages of group-aided decision processes.

II. Process:

Step 1. Individual Completion

Read the situation and complete the decision form quietly and individually.

Step 2. Form Groups

Form groups of approximately eight members—six participants and two observers. Each group will be assigned a number for purposes of identification.

Step 3. Consensus Guidelines

Your group is to employ the method of group consensus in reaching its decision. This means that the ranking for each of the twelve survival items must be agreed upon by each group member before it becomes a part of the group decision. Consensus is difficult to reach. Therefore, not every ranking will meet with everyone's complete approval. Try, as a group, to make each ranking one with which all group members can at least partially agree. Here are some guidelines to use in reaching consensus:

1. Avoid arguing blindly for your own opinions. Present your position as clearly and logically as possible, but listen to other members' reactions and consider them carefully before you press your point.

2. Avoid changing your mind just to reach agreement and avoid conflict. Support only solutions with which you are able to agree to at least some degree. Yield only to positions that have objective and logically sound foundations.

Step 4. Group Ranking

Decide upon a group ranking of the items on the decision form. Make a copy of the group ranking with your group designation clearly written at the top.

Step 5. Scoring

Score the individual decision forms in the following way:

1. Score the net (absolute) difference between the participant's answer and the correct answer. For example, if the participant's answer was 9 and the correct answer is 12, the net difference is 3. Disregard all plus or minus signs; find only the net difference for each item.

2. Total these scores; the result is the participant's score. The lower the score the more accurate the ranking.

3. To arrive at an average member score, total all members' scores for each group and divide by the number of members.

4. Put the scores in order from best to worst for each group. This ranking will be used to compare how many members, if any, had more accurate scores than the group's score.

5. In the summary table that follows the instruction sheets for the groups, enter the average member's score for each group and the score of the most accurate group member.

Step 6. Group Ranking

The groups complete their ranking with the group number or name clearly marked on the paper.

Step 7. Correct Ranking

Correct ranking provided.

Step 8. Class Discussion

Share the conclusions of each group in a general session.

WINTER SURVIVAL EXERCISE: THE SITUATION

Your university soccer team has just crash-landed in the woods of northern Minnesota and southern Manitoba. It is 11:32 a.m. in mid-January. The light plane in which you were traveling crashed on a lake. The pilot and copilot were killed. Shortly after the crash the plane sank completely into the lake with the pilot's and copilot's bodies inside. None of you are seriously injured and you are all dry.

The crash came suddenly, before the pilot had time to radio for help or inform anyone of your position. Since your pilot was trying to avoid a storm, you know the plane was considerably off course. The pilot announced shortly before the crash that you were twenty miles northwest of a small town that is the nearest known habitation.

You are in a wilderness area made up of thick woods broken by many lakes and streams.

The snow depth varies from above the ankles in windswept areas to knee-deep where it has drifted. The last weather report indicated that the temperature would reach minus twenty-five degrees Fahrenheit in the daytime and minus forty at night. There is plenty of dead wood and twigs in the immediate area. You are dressed in winter clothing appropriate for city wear—suits, pantsuits, street shoes, and overcoats. While escaping from the plane several members of your group salvaged twelve items.

Your task is to rank these items according to their importance to your survival, starting with 1 for the most important item and ending with 12 for the least important one. You may assume that the number of passengers is the same as the number of persons in your group, and that the group has agreed to stick together.

WINTER SURVIVAL DECISION FORM

Rank the following items according to their importance to your survival, starting with 1 for the most important one and proceeding to 12 for the least important one.

_____ Ball of steel wool

_____ Newspapers (one per person)

_____ Compass

_____ Hand ax

_____ Cigarette lighter (without fluid)

_____ Loaded .45-caliber pistol

_____ Sectional air map made of plastic

_____ Twenty-by-twenty-foot piece of heavy-duty canvas

_____ Extra shirt and pants for each survivor

_____ Can of shortening

_____ Quart of 100-proof whiskey

_____ Family-size chocolate bar (one per person)

WINTER SURVIVAL: GROUP SUMMARY SHEET

Item	Members						Summary
	1	2	3	4	5	6	
Ball of steel wool							
Newspapers							
Compass							
Hand ax							
Cigarette lighter							
.45-caliber pistol							
Sectional air map							
Canvas							
Shirts and pants							
Shortening							
Whiskey							
Chocolate bars							

Exercise Feedback Form

Chapter 12—Exercise 36

Name: _____ **Student ID:** _____

1. Was there anyone who had valuable information who could not persuade others to his or her point of view? If so, why?

2. What factors caused the group to use its resources well—or not well? Who behaved in what ways to influence group functioning?

3. Did anyone force his or her opinion on the group? If so, why was he or she able to do this?

You may be asked to complete and turn in this form to your instructor.

Chapter 13

Conflict, Power, and Politics

EXERCISE 37

Political Processes in Organizations

I. Objectives:

To analyze and predict when political behavior is used in organizational decision-making and to compare participants' ratings of politically-based decisions with ratings of practicing managers.

II. Process:

Step 1. Overview

Politics is the use of influence to make decisions and obtain preferred outcomes in organizations. Surveys of managers show that political behavior is a fact of life in virtually all organizations. In this exercise, you are asked to evaluate the extent to which politics will play a part in 11 types of decisions that are made in organizations.

Step 2. Individual Ranking

Rank the 11 organizational decisions listed on the scoring sheet according to the extent you think politics plays a part. The most political decision would be ranked 1, the least political decision would be ranked 11. Enter your ranking on the first column of the scoring sheet.

Step 3. Team Ranking

Your instructor will divide the class into groups. As a group, rank the 11 items according to your group's consensus on the amount of politics used in each decision. Use good group decision-making techniques to arrive at a consensus. Listen to each person's ideas and rationale fully before reaching a decision. Do not vote. Discuss items until agreement is reached. Base your decisions on the underlying logic provided by group members rather than on personal preference. After your team has reached a consensus, record the team rankings in the second column on the scoring sheet.

Step 4. Correct Ranking

After all groups have finished ranking the 11 decisions, your instructor will read the correct ranking based on a survey of managers. This survey indicates the frequency with which politics played a part in each type of decision. As the instructor reads each item's ranking, enter it in the "correct ranking" column on the scoring sheet.

Step 5. Individual Score

Your individual score is computed by taking the difference between your individual ranking and the correct ranking for each item. Be sure to use the *absolute* difference between your ranking and the correct ranking for each item (ignore pluses and minuses). Enter the difference in column 4 labeled "Individual Score." Add the numbers in column 4; this score indicates how accurate you were in assessing the extent to which politics plays a part in organizational decisions.

Step 6. Team Score

Compute the difference between your group's ranking and the correct ranking. Again, use the absolute difference for each item. Enter the difference in column 5 labeled "Team Score." Add the numbers in column 5; this total is your team score.

Step 7. Compare Teams and Class Discussion

When all individual and team scores have been calculated, the instructor may record the data from each group for class discussion.

SCORING SHEET

Decisions	1. Individual Ranking	2. Team Ranking	3. Correct Ranking	4. Individual Score	5. Team Score
1. Management promotions and transfers					
2. Entry level hiring					
3. Amount of pay					
4. Annual budgets					
5. Allocation of facilities, equipment, offices					
6. Delegation of authority among managers					
7. Interdepartmental coordination					
8. Specification of personnel policies					
9. Penalties for disciplinary infractions					
10. Performance appraisals					
11. Grievances and complaints					

Exercise Feedback Form

Chapter 13—Exercise 37

Name: _____   **Student ID:** _____

1. Why did some individuals and groups solve the ranking more accurately than others?

2. If the 11 decisions were ranked according to the importance of rational decision processes, how would that ranking compare to the one you completed in the exercise?

3. Is there any evidence from this exercise that would explain why more politics would appear at higher rather than lower levels in organizations?

EXERCISE 38

Conflict Strategies Exercise

I. Purpose:

To increase your awareness of what conflict strategies you use and how they compare with the strategies used by others.

II. Process:

Step 1. Complete Questionnaire

Working by yourself, complete the questionnaire entitled, "How You Act in Conflicts."

Step 2. Scoring Questionnaire

Score your questionnaire, using the scoring table on p. 207. Rank the five conflict strategies from the one you use the most to the one you use the least. This will give you an indication of how you see your own conflict strategy. The second most frequently used strategy is your backup strategy, the one you use if your first one fails.

How You Act in Conflicts

The items listed below can be thought of as descriptions of some of the different strategies for resolving conflicts. Read each of the items carefully. Using the following scale, indicate how typical each item is of your actions in a conflict.

5 = Strongly Agree 4 = Agree 3 = Neutral 2 = Disagree 1 = Strongly Disagree

_____ 1. I try to investigate an issue with my supervisor to find a solution acceptable to us.

_____ 2. I generally try to satisfy the needs of my supervisor.

_____ 3. I attempt to avoid being "put on the spot" and try to keep my conflict with my supervisor to myself.

_____ 4. I try to integrate my ideas with those of my supervisor to come up with a decision jointly.

_____ 5. I try to work with my supervisor to find solutions to a problem which satisfy our expectations.

_____ 6. I usually avoid open discussion of my differences with my supervisor.

_____ 7. I try to find a middle course to resolve an impasse.

_____ 8. I use my influence to get my ides accepted.

_____ 9. I use my authority to make a decision in my favor.

_____ 10. I usually accommodate the wishes of my supervisor.

_____ 11. I give in to the wishes of my supervisor.

_____ 12. I exchange accurate information with my supervisor to solve a problem together.

_____ 13. I usually allow concessions to my supervisor.

_____ 14. I usually propose a middle ground for breaking deadlocks.

_____ 15. I negotiate with my supervisor so that a compromise can be reached.

_____ 16. I try to stay away from disagreement with my supervisor.

_____ 17. I avoid an encounter with my supervisor.

_____ 18. I use my expertise to make a decision in my favor.

_____ 19. I often go along with the suggestions of my supervisor.

_____ 20. I use "give and take" so that a compromise can be made.

_____ 21. I am generally firm in pursuing my side of the issue.

_____ 22. I try to bring all our concerns out in the open so that the issues can be resolved in the best possible way.

_____ 23. I collaborate with my supervisor to come up with decisions acceptable to us.

_____ 24. I try to satisfy the expectations of my supervisor.

_____ 25. I sometimes use my power to win a competitive situation.

_____ 26. I try to keep my disagreement with my supervisor to myself in order to avoid hard feelings.

_____ 27. I try to avoid unpleasant exchanges with my supervisor.

_____ 28. I try to work with my supervisor for a proper understanding of a problem.

SCORING TABLE

Type I	Type II	Type III	Type IV	Type V
1.	2.	8.	3.	7.
4.	10.	9.	6.	14.
5.	11.	18.	16.	15.
12.	13.	21.	17.	20.
22.	19.	25.	26.	
23.	24.		27.	
28.				
Total ____	Total ____	Total ____	Total ____	Total ____
Divide by 7 Score = _____	Divide by 6 Score = _____	Divide by 5 Score = _____	Divide by 6 Score = _____	Divide by 4 Score = _____

Exercise Feedback Form

Chapter 13—Exercise 38

Name: _____ **Student ID:** _____

1. Does the conflict style identified by the exercise reflect the approach you take in conflict situations? Why or why not?

2. Did you have two scores that were high? The same? What conclusions do you make about the combinations of styles?

3. How would the style(s) identified by you influence your behavior in a conflict with a co-worker? A friend? A family member?

You may be asked to complete and turn in this form to your instructor.

EXERCISE 39

Prisoners' Dilemma: An Intergroup Competition

I. Objectives:

To explore trust between group members and effects of betrayal of trust, to demonstrate effects of interpersonal competition and to dramatize the merit of a collaborative posture in intragroup and intergroup relations.

II. Process:

Step 1. Form Teams

Two teams are formed and named Red and Blue. The teams are seated apart from each other. Teams are not to communicate with the each other in any way, verbally or nonverbally, except when told to do so by the facilitator.

Step 2. Review the Tally Sheet at the end of process steps, below.

Step 3. Round 1

Round 1 is begun. Teams have three minutes to make a team decision. Do not write your decisions until the instructor signals that time is up.

Step 4. Scoring

The choices of the two teams are announced for Round 1. The scoring for that round is agreed upon and is entered on the scorecard section of the Tally Sheet.

Step 5. Rounds 2 and 3

Rounds 2 and 3 are conducted in the same way as Round 1.

Step 6. Round 4

Round 4 is a special round, for which the payoff points are doubled. After representatives have conferred for three minutes, they return to their teams. Teams then have three minutes, as before, in which to make their decisions. When recording their scores, be sure that points indicated by the payoff schedule are doubled for this round only.

Step 7. Rounds 5–8

Rounds 5 through 8 are conducted in the same manner as the first three rounds.

Step 8. Round 9

Round 9 is a special round, in which the payoff points are "squared" (multiplied by themselves: e.g., a score of 4 would be $4^2 = 16$.) A minus sign should be retained: e.g., $(-3)^2 = -9$. Team representatives meet for three minutes; then, the teams meet for five minutes. At the instructor's signal, the teams write their choices; then the two choices are announced.

Step 9. Round 10

Round 10 is handled exactly as Round 9 was. Payoff points are squared.

Step 10. Concluding the Exercise

The entire group meets to process the experience. The point total for each team is announced, and the sum of the two team totals is calculated and compared to the maximum positive or negative outcomes (+126 or –126 points).

PRISONERS' DILEMMA TALLY SHEET

For ten successive rounds, the Red team will choose either an A or a B and the Blue Team will choose either an X or a Y. The score each team receives in a round is determined by the pattern made by the choices of both teams, according to the schedule below.

1. THE PAYOFF SCHEDULE

AX - Both teams win 3 points.
AY - Red Team loses 6 points; Blue Team wins 6 points.
BX - Red Team wins 6 points; Blue Team loses 6 points.
BY - Both teams lose 3 points.

2. THE SCORECARD

Round	Minutes	Choice		Cumulative Points	
		Red Team	Blue Team	Red Team	Blue Team
1	3				
2	3				
3	3				
4*	3 (reps.) 3 (teams)				
5	3				
6	3				
7	3				
8	3				
9**	3 (reps.) 3 (teams)				
10**	3 (reps.) 3 (teams)				

*   Payoff points are doubled for this round.

**   Payoff points are squared for this round; retain any minus signs.

Exercise Feedback Form

Chapter 13—Exercise 39

Name: _____ **Student ID:** _____

1. Did you worry about being betrayed in this exercise? If so, how did this make you feel?

2. What have you learned about trust in interpersonal, competitive relationships from this exercise?

3. Can you imagine situations where collaboration might not be the most useful approach? If so, what are these?

You may be asked to complete and turn in this form to your instructor.

Endnotes

Chapter 1: Organizations and Organization Theory

Exercise
1. Tosi, H.L. and Young, J.W. "Problem Solving Processes." *Management: Experience and Demonstrations.* 1-4, 1982. Homewood, Il: Richard D. Irwin, Inc. Reprinted by permission of the author.
2. McDonald, "International Exchange Game: A Hidden Social Dilemma" *Journal of Management Education*, 25 (4). 425-429, 2001, Reprinted by permission of Sage Publications, Inc.
3. England, G.W. and N.C. Agarwal. *The Manager and the Man: A Cross-Cultural Study of Personal Vales.* 29-32. 1974. Kent, OH: Kent State University Press.

Chapter 2: Strategy, Organization Design, and Effectiveness
4. Lewicki, R.J., D.D. Hall and F.S. Hall. "Organizational Diagnosis: Fast Food Technology." *Experience in Management and Organizational Behavior.* 224-227. 1998 New York: John Wiley and Sons, Inc.
5. Thomas, Joe G. "Examining Social Responsibility: A Trade-Off Among Stakeholders" *Journal of Management Education* 16. (2) 250-253, 1992. Reprinted by permission of Sage Publications.
6. Tosi, H.L. and J.W. Young. "Organizing Exercise #12." *Management: Experiences and Demonstrations.* 75-79, 1982. Homewood, IL: Richard D. Irwin, Inc.

Chapter 3: Fundamentals of Organization Structure
7. Daft, R.L. and K.M. Dahlen. "Creative Sentence Corporation." *Organization Theory: Cases and Applications.* 76-79. 1984, St. Paul, MN: West Publishing Company.
8. Daft, R.L. and K.M. Dahlen. "Creative Sentence Corporation." *Organization Theory: Cases and Applications.* 76-79. 1984, St. Paul, MN: West Publishing Company.
9. Harvey, Cheryl and Kim Morouney. "Organization Structure and Design: The Club Ed Exercise." *Journal of Management Education*, 22 (3) 425-429, 1998. Reprinted by permission of Sage Publications.

Chapter 4: The External Environment
10. Sashkin, Marshall; William C. Morris. *Organization Behavior: Concepts & Experience*, 1e. 1984, pp. 234-238. Reprinted by permission of Pearson Education, Inc. Upper Saddle River, NJ.
11. McGrath, Roger R. *Exercises in Management Fundamentals*, 1e. 1985, pp190-197. Reprinted by permission of Pearson Education, Inc. Upper Saddle River, NJ.

Chapter 5: Interorganizational Relationships
14. Mayer, Roger C. and Patricia M. Norman. "Exploring Attributes of Trustworthiness: A Classroom Exercise." *Journal of Management Education*, 28 (2) 224-249, 2004. Reprinted by permission of Sage Publications.
15. Grittner, Peter. "Four Elements of Successful Sourcing Strategies." *Management Review,* Vol. 85. 41-45, 1996.

Chapter 6: The International Environment and Organization Design
17. Paulson, Steven K. "Teaching International Business Concepts Through the Exchange of Cultural Metaphors." *Journal of Teaching in International Business*, Vol. 16 No. 4. 81-98. 2005.
18. Rarick, Charles A. "Moonbeam Electronics: Profiting from a Foreign Trade Zone." *Cases and Exercises in International Business.* 2003. Upper Saddle River, NJ. Reprinted by permission of the author.

Chapter 7: Manufacturing and Service Technologies
19. Withey, M.; Daft, R.L., and W.H. Cooper. "Measures of Perrow's Work Unit Technology: An Empirical Assessment and a New Scale." *Academy of Management Journal* 26 (1). 45-63, 1983. Reprinted by permission of Copyright Clearance Center.
20. Daft, R.L. "Relationships Among Interdependence and Other Characteristics of Team Play. (Exhibit 6-12)." *Organization Theory and Design* 222, 2001. Thomson/South-Western.

Chapter 8: Information Technology and Control

22. Leavitt, Harold J. and Ronald A.H. Muller. "Some Effects of Feedback on Communication." *Human Relations,* vol. IV, no. 4. 401-419.

23. http://marketingteacher.com/Lessons/lesson_balanced_scorecard.htm (Accessed 2/6/06). http://marketingteacher.com/Lessons/exercise_balanced_scorecard.htm (Accessed 2/6/06). http://marketingteacher.com/Lessons/answer_balanced_scorecard.htm (Accessed 2/6/06).

24. Baker III, Eugene A. and Kenneth M. Jennings. "An Out-of-Control Organizational Control Mechanism." *Journal of Management Education*, 18 (3). 380-384, 1994. Reprinted by Permission of Sage Publications, Inc.

Chapter 9: Organization Size, Life Cycle, and Decline

27. DuBrin, Andrew J. *Human Relations: A Job-Oriented Approach.* 434-435, 1992. Englewood Cliffs, NJ: Prentice Hall.

Chapter 10: Organizational Culture and Ethical Values

28. Landrum, Nancy E. "My Friend Morgan: An Exercise in Ethics." *Journal of Management Education*, 25 (3) 606-616. 2001. Reprinted by permission of Sage Publications, Inc.

29. Hames, David S. "Training in the Land of Doone: An Exercise in Cultural Differences." *Journal of Management Education*, 22 (3). 430-436, 1998. Reprinted by permission of Sage Publications, Inc.

30. "Case 1: Robin Hood." *Annual Editions: Management* 99/00. 43, 1999. Guilford, CT: Dushkin/McGraw-Hill.

Chapter 11: Innovation and Change

31. Baker III, H. Eugene. "Dynamics of Change: Precipitated Resistance to Change in the Classroom." *The Organizational Behavior Teaching Review* 13 (4). 134-137, 1988-89. Reprinted by permission of Sage Publications, Inc.

32. McDonald, K.S. and Mansour-Cole, D. "Change requires intensive care: An experiential exercise for learners in university and corporate settings." *Journal of Management Education,* 24 (1). 127-148, 2000. Reprinted by permission of Sage Publications, Inc.

33. Barbuto, Jr., John E. "Power and the Changing Environment." *Journal of Management Education*, 24 (2). 288-296, 2000. Reprinted by permission of Sage Publications, Inc.

Chapter 12: Decision Making Processes

34. Tosi, H.L and J.W. Young. "Decision Making Exercise #26." *Management: Experiences and Demonstrations.* 159-164, 1982. Homewood, IL: Richard D. Irwin, Inc. Reprinted by permission of the author.

35. Mallinger, Mark. "Decisive Decision Making: An Exercise Using Ethical Frameworks." *Journal of Management Education*, 21 (3). 411-417, 1997. Reprinted by Permission of Sage Publications, Inc.

36. Johnson, D.W. and F.P. Johnson. "Winter Survival Exercise." *Joining Together: Group Theory & Group Skills*, 2e. Published by Allyn & Bacon, Boston, MA. ©1982 by Pearson Education. Reprinted by permission of the publisher.

Chapter 13: Conflict, Power, and Politics

37. Daft, R.L. and M.P. Sharfman. "Political Processes in Organizations." *Organization Theory: Cases and Applications.* 339-341, 1990. St. Paul, MN: West Publishing Company.

38. Rahim, M.A. and N.R. Mace. "Confirmatory Factor Analysis of the Styles of Handling Interpersonal Conflict: First-Order Factor Model and Its Invariance Across Groups." *Journal of Applied Psychology*, 80 (1). 122-132, 1995.

39. Pfeiffer, J.W. and J.E. Jones (Eds.). "Prisoner's Dilemma: An Intergroup Competition." *A Handbook of Structured Experiences for Human Relations Training.* 52-56, 1974. San Diego, CA: Pfeiffer and Company.